Cloning

Other Books of Related Interest:

Opposing Viewpoints Series

Biomedical Ethics

Cloning

Ethics

Genetic Engineering

Health

Humanity's Future

Technology and Society

Current Controversies Series

Ethics

Genetic Engineering

Medical Ethics

At Issue Series

Cloning

The Ethics of Human Cloning

Gene Therapy

Human Embryo Experimentation

Reproductive Technology

Cloning

Sylvia Engdahl, Book Editor

GREENHAVEN PRESS

An imprint of Thomson Gale, a part of The Thomson Corporation

Detroit • New York • San Francisco • San Diego • New Haven, Conn.
Waterville, Maine • London • Munich

THOMSON
™
GALE

Bonnie Szumski, *Publisher*
Helen Cothran, *Managing Editor*
David M. Haugen, *Series Editor*

© 2006 Thomson Gale, a part of The Thomson Corporation.

Thomson and Star Logo are trademarks and Gale and Greenhaven Press are registered trademarks used herein under license.

For more information, contact:
Greenhaven Press
27500 Drake Rd.
Farmington Hills, MI 48331-3535
Or you can visit our Internet site at http://www.gale.com

Articles in Greenhaven Press anthologies are often edited for length to meet page requirements. In addition, original titles of these works are changed to clearly present the main thesis and to explicitly indicate the author's opinion. Every effort is made to ensure that Greenhaven Press accurately reflects the original intent of the authors. Every effort has been made to trace the owners of copyrighted material.

Cover photograph reproduced by permission of © Jim Richardson/CORBIS.

LIBRARY OF CONGRESS CATALOGING-IN-PUBLICATION DATA

Cloning / Sylvia Engdahl, book editor
   p. cm. -- (Contemporary issues companion)
   Includes bibliographical references and index.
   0-7377-2771-3 (lib. : alk. paper) 0-7377-2772-1 (pbk. : alk. paper)
   1. Cloning. 2. Cloning--Social aspects. I. Engdahl, Sylvia Louise. II. Series.
   QH442.2.C5647 2006
   174'.957--dc22

                     2005055062

Printed in the United States of America
10 9 8 7 6 5 4 3 2 1

Contents

Chapter 3: Therapeutic Cloning of Human Embryos for Medical Research

Chapter 4: The Prospect of Human Reproductive Cloning

Foreword

In the news, on the streets, and in neighborhoods, individuals are confronted with a variety of social problems. Such problems may affect people directly: A young woman may struggle with depression, suspect a friend of having bulimia, or watch a loved one battle cancer. And even the issues that do not directly affect her private life—such as religious cults, domestic violence, or legalized gambling—still impact the larger society in which she lives. Discovering and analyzing the complexities of issues that encompass communal and societal realms as well as the world of personal experience is a valuable educational goal in the modern world.

Effectively addressing social problems requires familiarity with a constantly changing stream of data. Becoming well informed about today's controversies is an intricate process that often involves reading myriad primary and secondary sources, analyzing political debates, weighing various experts' opinions—even listening to firsthand accounts of those directly affected by the issue. For students and general observers, this can be a daunting task because of the sheer volume of information available in books, periodicals, on the evening news, and on the Internet. Researching the consequences of legalized gambling, for example, might entail sifting through congressional testimony on gambling's societal effects, examining private studies on Indian gaming, perusing numerous Web sites devoted to Internet betting, and reading essays written by lottery winners as well as interviews with recovering compulsive gamblers. Obtaining valuable information can be time-consuming—since it often requires researchers to pore over numerous documents and commentaries before discovering a source relevant to their particular investigation.

Greenhaven's Contemporary Issues Companion series seeks to assist this process of research by providing readers with useful and pertinent information about today's complex issues. Each volume in this anthology series focuses on a topic of current interest, presenting informative and thought-provoking selections written from a wide variety of viewpoints. The readings selected by the editors include such diverse sources as personal accounts and case studies, pertinent factual and statistical articles, and relevant commentaries and overviews. This diversity of sources and views, found in every Contemporary Issues Companion, offers readers a broad perspective in one convenient volume.

In addition, each title in the Contemporary Issues Companion series is designed especially for young adults. The selections included in every volume are chosen for their accessibility and are expertly edited in consideration of both the reading and comprehension levels of the audience. The structure of the anthologies also enhances accessibility. An introductory essay places each issue in context and provides helpful facts such as historical background or current statistics and legislation that pertain to the topic. The chapters that follow organize the material and focus on specific aspects of the book's topic. Every essay is introduced by a brief summary of its main points and biographical information about the author. These summaries aid in comprehension and can also serve to direct readers to material of immediate interest and need. Finally, a comprehensive index allows readers to efficiently scan and locate content.

The Contemporary Issues Companion series is an ideal launching point for research on a particular topic. Each anthology in the series is composed of readings taken from an extensive gamut of resources, including periodicals, newspapers, books, government documents, the publications of private and public organizations, and Internet Web sites. In these volumes, readers will find factual support suitable for use in reports, debates, speeches, and research papers. The anthologies also facilitate further research, featuring a book and periodical bibliography and a list of organizations to contact for additional information.

A perfect resource for both students and the general reader, Greenhaven's Contemporary Issues Companion series is sure to be a valued source of current, readable information on social problems that interest young adults. It is the editors' hope that readers will find the Contemporary Issues Companion series useful as a starting point to formulate their own opinions about and answers to the complex issues of the present day.

Introduction

Today, people do not have to be science fiction enthusiasts to know—or think they know—what human cloning is. Since 1997, when the cloning of Dolly the sheep was announced, the media have given plenty of attention to the subject. Nevertheless, the general public's idea of clones has been formed on the basis of the way they are portrayed in science fiction movies. Many scientists believe that this is unfortunate because that portrayal is almost always contrary to the scientific facts about cloning.

The 2005 movie *The Island*, for instance, reiterates several common misconceptions. In the first place, its premise is that adult human clones would be used as "spare parts" for people needing replacement organs. Geneticists agree that this could never happen, not only because a cloned person would have human rights but because it would be a needlessly complex way of producing cloned organs. Someday, it may indeed become technologically possible to clone human organs for medical use—but those organs would be grown separately, outside the body. There would be no point in going to the trouble and expense of producing cloned people for such a use; no one outside science fiction has suggested that anything could be gained by it.

Cloning experts also point to other major fallacies in *The Island* and in many other movies, such as *Attack of the Clones*, *The Sixth Day*, and *Multiplicity*. In all of these films, clones are shown being created in a relatively short time, as adults; in some of the movies, a lot of identical ones are produced. However, scientists explain that cloning could not work that way. Cloning is possible only at the embryo stage. A cloned person would be born like any other baby and would take just as long to reach adulthood. Furthermore, in some of these films, it is stated that a clone would have the memories of the person he or she was cloned from. That, geneticists say, is impossible. Cloning is a process that copies DNA—genes—not qualities that have been acquired during the DNA donor's lifetime.

Because cloning copies only DNA, cloned people would not be identical to the people from whose cells they were reproduced. All scientists agree that the characteristics of a person depend not only on genes, but on the environment in which he or she develops and continues to live—the prenatal environment as well as the experiences undergone after birth. The 1978 movie *The Boys from Brazil* takes this into account; in it, the evil Nazi hoping to re-create Hitler exposes cloned children to some of the things Hitler experienced as a child. To scientists, however, this is a very crude, oversimplified conception of environment. In reality, every minor detail a person (even an infant) sees, hears, feels, or thinks is part of that person's environment. Just as identical twins raised together are not identical in their abilities, interests, and personalities, clones—who were not born at the same time and whose experiences were even less similar than those of twins—would not be replicas of their DNA donors, cloning experts insist. It is therefore scientifically meaningless to wonder whether someone like Hitler will ever succeed in creating duplicates. Experts also contend that it is equally meaningless to wonder whether a duplicate of a gifted person or a loved one can ever be created by cloning. The extent to which genes influence personality is controversial, but it is known that they do not wholly determine it.

Reproduction by means of cloning is already being done commercially with cats. In the 2000 movie *The Sixth Day*, a fictional pet cloning company called RePet promises, "Should accident, illness or age end your pet's natural life, our proven genetic technology can have him or her back the same day, in perfect health, with zero defects, guaranteed." On the other hand, a real pet cloning company, Genetic Savings & Clone, states, "We decline business from people who want us to bring specific pets back to life. Nobody can do that. Our goal is to produce new pets possessing the same genes as previous pets.... Of course a clone doesn't inherit the memories and experiences of its genetic donor; it's a unique individual, like an identical twin born later. But if a clone is raised in a similar way as its genetic donor, you'll probably see behavioral similarities." In the movie, the pets, like most human clones in science fiction, come to life immediately as adults, whereas real cloned cats are implanted into the wombs of surrogate mothers and are born as kittens; they cannot be given to their owners until they are weaned. Scientists expect that in the future, when more pets have been cloned and have grown into mature adults, more people will begin to realize that clones are not exact copies of the originals that donated their genes.

The presentation of cloning in movies has been overwhelmingly negative. To be sure, in some movies clones are used in a symbolic way: as a metaphor for uniformity, as commentary on the willingness of some people to exploit others for their personal benefit, or—for example, in *Godsend*—as a warning about the futility of trying to bring back the dead. The creators of these films did not intend them to be taken literally, but the public nevertheless often forms its opinions about clones on the basis of the fiction in which clones have been featured. The very term *clone* has acquired such negative associations that some bioethicists feel it should not be used as a noun in reference to cloned persons. Gregory Pence, for example, compares it to terms used by bigots for minorities and writes, "'Clone' by now connotes aberrant, mass-produced, commodified subhumans. It is a deeply prejudicial term."

The view of most people toward the possibility of human reproductive cloning—that is, cloning to make babies as distinguished from the cloning of tissues for medical use—has been overwhelmingly negative, too. The majority of individuals and organizations who favor therapeutic (medical) cloning are very careful to make plain that they are opposed to human reproductive cloning. And there are, in fact, some strong reasons for opposition. However, knowledgeable opponents of cloning do not base their arguments on the false stereotypes about clones promoted by Hollywood. Instead, they consider problems that might really arise if some babies were created through cloning instead of through the union of male and female reproductive cells.

Although it is true that until recently the public was almost unanimously against human reproductive cloning, that is changing. A minority now believes it is inevitable and may have legitimate uses. Many experts feel that cloning humans is an inherently repugnant idea and maintain that it should be banned, even though they recognize that clones would not be as much like their genetic donors as has been assumed. Others think, however, that if it becomes safe—which at present, it is not—prevailing attitudes will change, just as has occurred with in vitro fertilization: the development of "test-tube babies." Advocates of cloning assert that cloned people would not be biologically different from other people; only their origin would be different. Whether this would be psychologically harmful to them, or to society, is something about which authorities as yet do not agree.

CHAPTER 1

Public Attitudes
Toward Cloning

What Is a Clone?

Jay D. Gralla and Preston Gralla

Jay D. Gralla is a professor of biochemistry and molecular biology at UCLA. Preston Gralla is a well-known technology expert and columnist who has written many books. In the following selection from their book The Complete Idiot's Guide to Understanding Cloning, *they present basic information about how plants and animals are cloned. Cloning is not new, they explain, because nature has been cloning plants for millions of years and some forms of animal life can clone themselves. In addition, scientists cloned salamanders and frogs in the early and mid-twentieth century. But the possibility of cloning did not become familiar to the general public until the first cloning of a mammal, Dolly the sheep, was announced in 1997.*

So what is a clone? Put simply, it's a copy of another organism that has the exact same DNA as the original.

Cloning is nothing new—nature has been doing it for millions of years. When plants like strawberry plants and potatoes send out runners, modified versions of a stem, new plants grow wherever the runners take root. Each new plant is a clone of the original.

Certain animals can clone themselves. A tiny water animal called the hydra can clone an entire new identical hydra from the original when a small part is cut off. That small part grows an entire new hydra with the exact same genetic material as the original.

Even higher-level animals, under certain conditions, can to a certain extent clone themselves through a process called *parthenogenesis*. Some animals, such as certain insects, worms,

Jay D. Gralla and Preston Gralla, *The Complete Idiot's Guide to Understanding Cloning.* New York: Alpha Books, 2004. Copyright © 2004 by Jay D. Gralla and Preston Gralla. Reproduced by permission of Alpha Books, an imprint of Penguin Group (USA) Inc.

and some species of lizards, fish, and frogs, can develop into adults from unfertilized eggs, in certain environments. Each of the animals that develops will get genetic material only from the mother, and none from the father.

The most obvious example of cloning is human identical twins. . . . When an egg is fertilized by a sperm, the new cell gets half of its chromosomes from the sperm and half from the egg. That fertilized egg begins to divide and all the cells have the exact same chromosomes as the original egg. It turns into an embryo, and the embryo then develops into a person.

However, if the fertilized egg splits into two identical cells, each of those cells can develop into an embryo and turn into a person. Because the two initial cells have the identical DNA, the resulting twins have the identical DNA. The result: identical twins.

Nature has been busy cloning organisms for a long time, but only in more recent times has man gotten into the act. The big breakthrough, of course, was when Dolly the sheep was cloned in 1997. But we have been cloning plants and animals for a long time before then—in fact, when it comes to plants, we've been cloning for thousands of years. Much agriculture is based on cloning. . . .

How Plants Are Cloned

You may not realize it, but if you've worked with plants at all, you've probably done some cloning. The technique is about as simple as it gets. Take a leaf cutting from a plant, help it grow roots, and then replant it. Congratulations! It's your first clone! That new plant has the identical DNA to the original plant from which you took it, and so is a clone of it. This technique is called *vegetative propagation*, and has been used for millennia.

This technique may be second nature to you, and seem rather mundane, but if you stop and think about it for a moment, you'll realize just how amazing it is. The leaf starts off only as a leaf, but it is able to grow entirely new structures—roots and stems—and turn into an entire new plant. . . .

How Animals Are Cloned

When it comes to cloning, plants are easy—animals are hard. After all, we've been cloning plants for millennia, but we've only just gotten around to cloning animals.

Most people have heard of the cloned sheep Dolly, but cloning didn't start with Dolly. In 1902 the German embryologist Hans Spemann used a strand of hair as a kind of noose and split apart the cells of a two-celled salamander embryo. Each embryo then developed into a full-grown salamander, and each was a clone of the original embryo. In essence, Spemann had induced artificial twinning, mimicking the way that twins are created in nature.

Based on his experiments, Spemann suggested that a "fantastical experiment" be conducted in which an organism would be cloned by transferring nuclear material into an egg. The technology of the time didn't allow that experiment to be done. But in 1952, two scientists, Robert Briggs and Thomas King, were in fact able to do it. They extracted the nucleus from the cells of one frog, and inserted it into an egg cell of another frog whose nucleus had been taken out. The end result: A cloned frog.

In the experiment, the nucleus that was inserted into the egg was taken from an undifferentiated cell from a developing embryo. Undifferentiated cells have the capability to grow into many different kinds of cells. Robert Briggs and Thomas King thought that nuclei from adult cells could never be used to create clones.

Alas, Briggs and King were wrong in their prediction. John Gurdon was able to take the nucleus from an adult skin cell of a frog, and transplant it into a nuclear-less egg from a second frog. . . . The result: A tadpole that is the clone of the frog that donated the nucleus.

Let's take a closer look at how it works, because the general technique is used commonly in cloning.

First, an egg is extracted from an adult frog (which we'll call frog A), and radiation is used to destroy the frog's nucleus. The resulting egg is called an enucleated egg—one without a nucleus.

Next, a cell is extracted from an adult frog (which we'll call frog B)—in this instance, from a skin cell. The nucleus is extracted from the cell, and is then implanted into the enucleated egg. The egg now has the nucleus of frog B, which contains all of frog B's DNA. The egg becomes an embryo and develops into a tadpole, and because the tadpole has the DNA from frog B, it is a clone from frog B.

How Dolly Was Cloned

Gurdon's frog experiments didn't make that big a splash in the world—few people in the general public had heard about them.

But when the sheep named Dolly was cloned, it made front-page headlines all over the world. Not only had a mammal been successfully cloned for the first time, but the implications were clear: If a sheep could be cloned, why not humans?

Dolly was cloned at the Edinburgh-based Roslin Institute by a team led by professor Ian Wilmut through a technique known as *nuclear transfer*. Dolly was cloned not for purely theoretical reasons. Wilmut wanted to genetically engineer sheep and other farm animals so that they could produce proteins in their milk that could help humans—for example, insulin.

The path was not easy. They attempted to make a clone 276 times and it failed each time. Only on the 277th try did they succeed. Talk about perseverance.

The technique used to clone Dolly builds on Gurdon's experiments with frogs, but takes it several steps beyond. One of the key challenges was to "reprogram" the DNA of the cell that donates the nucleus—the cell that will be cloned. The problem the group faced is that adult cells are programmed to perform certain functions, for example, skin cells are programmed to grow new skin over a wound. They're not programmed to do other things, such as turn into a heart tissue or lung tissue or kidney tissue.

A newly fertilized egg cell contains undifferentiated cells—they can turn into any kind of cell in the human body. So taking the DNA from a differentiated cell of an adult, like a skin cell, and placing it into an egg cell has serious potential problems. The DNA isn't programmed to turn into other kinds of cells, and so the egg cell won't be able to divide successfully, turn into an embryo, and then ultimately turn into an adult animal.

Reprogramming the DNA

So you have to "reprogram" the nucleus of that adult cell so that it doesn't just produce skin, for example—it has to be able to produce any kind of skin in the body.

Here's how they solved the problem. As with the experiment with frogs, two cells were required: an adult cell, whose DNA would be used; and an egg cell, which would be the recipient of the DNA.

An egg cell was taken from a Scottish Blackface sheep (which as its name implied, has a black face) shortly after the sheep ovulated. The egg cell was taken then because that was the time that it would be most susceptible to fertilization. An instrument called a pipette was then used to remove the nucleus of the egg cell. The end result was an egg that had not yet been fertilized, and that had no nucleus in it—which means that it had no chromosomes. By itself, it could do nothing.

Then an adult cell was taken from the mammary gland of an udder of a Finn Dorset sheep, that is completely white. The

21

cell was taken from the udder because during pregnancy udder cells grow rapidly. The cell was put in a Petri dish and "starved"—it was denied nutrients that would allow it to grow and divide. Of course, it wasn't completely starved, or else it would die. But it was starved enough to put it into a suspended state. In this way, its state matched the state of the enucleated egg, which was also in a suspended state of sorts because it lacked DNA.

Next, the two cells were placed next to one another, and electricity was used to jolt the cells into merging into a single cell. Once the cells merged into one, another jolt was used to get the new, merged cell to begin dividing. This mimicked the natural burst of energy that accompanies the fertilization of an egg cell by a sperm cell.

The cell now began dividing like any other embryo. After about a week it was implanted into the uterus of a surrogate mother sheep, which was also a Blackface ewe. Why put it into a Blackface ewe, and why have the egg come from a Blackface ewe and the DNA from a white Finn Dorset sheep? So that it would be abundantly clear where the DNA of the resulting clone came from. If the clone turned out to be all-white, its DNA would very obviously be from the Finn Dorset; if it had a black face, it would come from the Blackface ewe. Of course, a DNA test would be able to prove that as well, but DNA tests don't look good on TV. The ultimate result? Dolly, the world's first mammal clone. Its DNA was identical to the DNA of the Finn Dorsett sheep that donated the nucleus.

Since Dolly was cloned, scientists have cloned a veritable menagerie of animals. Mice, cattle, pigs, cats, rodents ... the list goes on and on. For example, a domestic calico cat was cloned, and given the name Carbon Copy.

One of the more intriguing recent clones was of a racing mule. (Yes, there are such things.) This is unusual because mules are sterile—they don't produce offspring. They are the result of a union of a horse and a donkey. In the process, first a donkey and a horse were bred and the fetus allowed to grow. Researchers then took the DNA from the fetus, and implanted it into the enucleated egg from a horse. The resulting eggs were placed into the womb of a female horse, and the end result was a cloned mule.

Clones Are Not Exact Copies

A clone has the exact same genome as the animal or plant from which it is cloned. That doesn't mean, however, that the animal or plant will turn out to be identical to the original. In fact, very often, that is not the case.

Environmental factors affect how organisms turn out to a great degree—as anyone who has followed the nature-or-nurture debate knows. Even human twins raised in the same family end up looking and acting differently as they grow older. One may be heavier than the other, or more athletically talented, or shyer, for example.

The cloned cat Carbon Copy is a perfect example of this. Carbon Copy was a calico cat, as was the cat from which it was cloned. Calico cats have distinctive coat patterns made up of orange, black, and white colors. Yet the calico pattern of Carbon Copy differed from that of the cat from which it was cloned. Although genes made the cat a calico one, other factors decided exactly how that calico pattern looked.

There are other reasons why clones are not actually exact copies. Although cloned DNA always has the same sequence, that DNA doesn't always act the same. There are several reasons for this. One is that the donated cell nucleus already contains some proteins and these proteins influence which genes are actually expressed. So, nuclei donated from two different types of cells from the exact same donor could give somewhat different features to clones even though they contain the very same DNA sequence. Secondly, small chemicals can attach to and imprint the DNA. These chemical attachments differ from cell to cell and can alter how genes are expressed. And the egg contains its own set of proteins that also influence how genes are expressed.

Moreover, the egg does contain some DNA that is not part of the chromosomes. . . . Cells contain mitochondria—the cell's power station. Well, mitochondria have their own DNA, and these contain genes that power the cell. So the clone does have a little piece of DNA from its mother. In fact, whether you're a man or a woman, your mitochondrial DNA power-house came from your mother. . . .

Cloned Animals Often Have Health Problems

Many . . . cloned animals face premature deaths and health problems. For example, Japanese researchers cloned mice and compared their life spans with a control group of mice that were the result of natural birth and in vitro fertilization. After 800 days, 83 percent of the cloned mice had died, but only 23 percent of the control group had died. The cloned mice died prematurely from tumors, damaged livers, and pneumonia.

And a group at the Whitehead Institute for Biomedical Research in Cambridge, Massachusetts studied 10,000 genes in the livers and placentas of cloned mice. They discovered that hundreds of the genes had abnormal activity patterns.

Those are just a few examples; many researchers report similar findings.

No one is quite sure why all this happens. In addition to the problem of "old" DNA, there may be other issues as well. The truth is, normal dividing eggs and embryos grow under extraordinarily complex, constantly changing chemical conditions in which gene activity is turned on and off. Embryo division is activated and enhanced by changes in calcium levels, for example, as well as by a chemical called *oscillin* brought into the embryo by the sperm. In cloning, there is no fertilization, and the egg begins to divide in dishes rather than in fallopian tubes and the uterus.

Scientists have even found out that cloned embryos and normal embryos have different nutritional needs. Keith Latham, an associate professor in the Fels Institute for Cancer Research and Molecular Biology at Temple University in Philadelphia, discovered that mouse clone embryos do best when fed glucose, while normal mouse embryos do better with other kinds of sugars.

Many scientists also point out that the problems may be tied to the "reprogramming" that needs to be done in the DNA from adult cells. No one knows what the effects of that reprogramming are.

Dolly Is a Symbol of the Public's Ideas About Cloning

Dorothy Nelkin and M. Susan Lindee

The late Dorothy Nelkin was a sociologist on the faculty of New York University and the author of many books about technology and society. M. Susan Lindee is a historian of science at the University of Pennsylvania. They coauthored The DNA Mystique: The Gene as a Cultural Icon. *In the following selection they discuss the public reaction to the cloning of Dolly the sheep, who died in 2003. They explain that Dolly has become a symbol not only of what people think about cloning in general—including the possibility of cloning humans—but of popular beliefs about human nature, the social order, and the power of new technologies to shape the future.*

Dolly [was] a cloned sheep born in July 1996 at the Roslin Institute in Edinburgh by Ian Wilmut, a British embryologist. She was produced, after 276 failed attempts, from the genetic material of a six-year-old sheep. But Dolly is also a Rorschach test. The public response to the production of a lamb from an adult cell mirrors the futuristic fantasies and Frankenstein fears that have more broadly surrounded research in genetics, and especially genetic engineering. Dolly stands in for other monstrosities—both actual and fictional—that human knowledge and technique have produced. She provokes fear not so much because she [was] novel, but because she [was] such a familiar entity: a biological product of human design who appears to be a human surrogate. Dolly as "virtual" person is terrifying and seductive—despite her placid temperament.

Cloning was a term originally applied to a botanical technique of asexual reproduction. But following early experiments in the manipulation of hereditary and reproductive processes during the mid-1960s, the term became associated with human biological engineering. It also became a pervasive theme in horror films and science fiction fantasies. Appearing to promise both new control over nature and dehumanization, cloning attracted significant popular attention.

Genetic Essentialism: A Popular Misconception

Underlying many depictions of cloning is the idea that human beings in all their complexity are simply readouts of a powerful molecular text. In *The DNA Mystique: The Gene as a Cultural Icon*, we called this idea *genetic essentialism*, a deterministic tendency to reduce personality and behavior to the genes. Exploring the popular appeal of genetic essentialism, we tracked its manifestations in the mass media—in television programs, advertising and marketing media, newspaper articles, films, child-care books, and popular magazines. We found repeated messages suggesting that the personal characteristics and identity of individuals are entirely encoded in a molecular text. We found references to genes for criminality, shyness, arson, directional ability, exhibitionism, tendencies to tease, social potency, sexual preferences, job success, divorce, religiosity, political leanings, traditionalism, zest for life, and preferred styles of dressing. We found pleasure-seeking genes, celebrity genes, couch-potato genes, genes for saving, and even genes for sinning. And we documented the public fears—or sometimes hopes—that geneticists will soon acquire the awesome power to manipulate the molecular text and thereby to determine the human future.

The responses to the Dolly phenomenon reflected these ideas. Dolly and cloning were immediately the subject of jokes on late-night talk shows and Internet web sites. Their humor depended largely on the assumption that human identity is contained entirely in the sequences of DNA in the human genome: Why not clone great athletes like Michael Jordan, or great scientists like Albert Einstein, or popular politicians like Tony Blair, or less popular politicians like Newt Gingrich, or wealthy entrepreneurs like Bill Gates? But there were also many anxious scenarios in the popular press, including futuristic stories about making new Frankenstein monsters, or creating Adolf Hitler clones, or producing "organ donors" only to harvest their (fully compatible) viscera.

Dolly seems to lead to a future of highly managed, commercialized bodies both animal and human. She is a manifestation of scientific rationality—a machine that can be tailored to human needs. And she is a symbol of human vulnerability—a sign that males may become obsolete or that commercial interests will dictate the human future. Speculations about Dolly reveal the patterns of current perceptions of science in the biotechnology age.

Views of Cloning Are Influenced by Science Fiction

Cloning has long been a theme in novels and science fiction films. Most of these stories tend to be traditional narratives of divine retribution for violating the sanctity of human life. These days they employ the language of genetics, and they often dwell on the horrible consequences of genetic manipulation. . . .

In 1993, scientists from George Washington University [GWU] "twinned" a nonviable human embryo in an experiment intended to create embryos for in vitro fertilization. When they reported their work at the meeting of the American Fertility Society, newspapers, magazines, and television talk shows covered the experiment as if it involved a cloning technology for the mass production of human beings. While the scientists viewed their research as a contribution to helping infertile patients, the media stories about the research envisioned selective breeding factories, cloning on consumer demand, the breeding of children as organ donors, a cloning industry for selling multiples of human beings, and even a freezer section of the "biomarket." Journalists anticipated a "Brave New World of cookie cutter humans," and they asked if the GWU scientists were playing God. A *Time* magazine survey found that 75% of their respondents thought cloning was not a good thing, and 58% thought it was morally wrong. Thirty-seven percent wanted research on cloning to be banned; 40% called for a temporary halt to research.

Some Views of Cloning Are Positive

Yet, public responses to the GWU experiment in 1993 and then to Wilmut's experiment four years later were not all so negative. For some, cloning held the promise of creating perfect cows, sheep, and chickens, or perhaps even perfect people. Reflecting deterministic assumptions of genetic essentialism, media stories have suggested that clones would surely be identical products of their genes.

Reproduction has often appeared in mass media stories as a commercial transaction where the goal is to produce good stock. Sperm banks are described as a place to shop for "Mr. Good Genes" where potential parents scan lists of desirable genetic traits. Why not, in this context, use cloning to produce and reproduce perfect babies? They could, after all, be dependable reproductive products with proven performance.

Cloning has also been viewed as a way to assure a kind of immortality. Scientists have commonly constructed DNA as an immortal text. The Human Genome Diversity Project seeks to "immortalize" vanishing populations through saving their DNA. Molecular biologists have tried to extract "immortal" DNA from the remains of historical figures such as Abraham Lincoln and to reconstruct their health and personal characteristics long after they are dead. In his popular book *The Self-*

ish Gene, sociobiologist Richard Dawkins argues that DNA is immortalized through the reproductive process, for we are blindly programmed to preserve and pass on our genes. And, of course, in *Jurassic Park,* the DNA lives on forever in fossilized form and contains the complete instruction code of the living organism. In Michael Crichton's story, if you want a dinosaur, all you need is dinosaur DNA.

Post-Dolly narratives build on these assumptions. Again and again media stories have predicted that cloning will allow the resurrection of the dead (bereaved parents, for example, might clone a beloved deceased child). Or the technology could provide life everlasting for the deserving (narcissists could arrange to have themselves cloned). Dawkins confessed his own desire to be cloned: "I think it would be mind-bogglingly fascinating to watch a younger edition of myself growing up in the twenty-first century instead of the 1940s." Indeed, psychiatrist Robert Coles, in a *New York Times* interview, suggested that the very idea of cloning "tempts our narcissism enormously because it gives a physical dimension to a fantasy that one can keep going on through the reproduction of oneself."

Not surprisingly, in the United States, where demands and desires are frequently framed in terms of rights, cloning too has been defined as a "right." Infertile women and their physicians have been among the most ardent advocates of cloning as a right; for if a single embryo could be used to create identical embryos for later fertilization, this could avoid the hormonal overload and painful procedures that women undergo for in vitro fertilization. The technology of cloning thus spawned not only Dolly but an association called "Cloning Rights United Front." Its members insisted that cloning is part of the reproductive rights of every human being, and, in tune with the political sentiments of the 1990s, they wanted "the government to keep out." . . .

Technical Details vs. Symbolic Associations

In his scientific paper itself, Wilmut fussed over the problem of whether "a differentiated adult nucleus can be fully reprogrammed." He called the lamb in question 6LL3 rather than Dolly, and made it clear, in diagrams and illustrations of gels, that there is some question about the precise genetic relationship between Dolly and the "donor." Somatic DNA, which was the source of Dolly's genes, is constantly mutating. Dolly, in fact, may not be genetically identical in every way to her "mother," a point that is of some importance for the possible agricultural uses of cloning techniques.

For writers in the popular press, however, such technical details were less important than symbolic associations. The cloning of a lamb was immediately set in a context of other fears about genetics and genetic manipulation, and especially about rapid and sometimes startling advances in reproductive technology. The technological changes allowed by the possibility of freezing sperm and embryos and by the improvements in techniques of in vitro [outside the body] fertilization (IVF) have been remarkable. But they have also been controversial. They have included, for example, a controversial proposal, put forth by a fertility specialist, to harvest eggs from the ovaries of aborted fetuses and then mature the fetal cells and fertilize them in a petri dish for use in research and implantation. And they have included a plan for creating embryos through parthenogenesis. The debates over such reproductive techniques set the stage for the response to cloning.

So too, responses to Dolly reflected public debates about other uses and abuses of science and technology. One journalist compared cloning to weapons development. Another worried that the shortage of organs for transplantation would be resolved by cloning anencephalic babies (who are born without a brain but are otherwise normal), so that their organs could be harvested for patients in need. Many news stories have reflected mistrust of scientists, and the fear that the outrageous possibilities suggested by cloning a sheep will eventually, perhaps inevitably, be realized in human beings. News headlines frequently suggest that science cannot be controlled: "Science Fiction Has Become a Social Reality." "Whatever's Next?" And, of course, "Pandora's Box."

Cloning and Commercialization

Many news and popular culture accounts have expressed the growing tensions over commercial trends in genetics and biotechnology and their implications for the commodification of the body. A series of legal developments in the 1980s set the stage for commercial developments in biotechnology. They encouraged collaborations between university researchers and biotechnology companies and allowed the patenting of products of nature, including human genes. In this context, business interests welcomed Dolly; for cloning has huge potential economic implications especially for agricultural and pharmaceutical applications. As predicted by a *Business Week* cover article in March 1997, called "The Biotech Century," "cloning animals is just the beginning." Such advances "will define progress in the 21st century. It's all happening faster than anyone expected."

But there is a downside of these commercial trends that also helped to shape responses to the cloning experiments. Critics have documented the growing conflicts of interest in science, the increased secrecy, and the reluctance to share data. Reporters noted that Wilmut held back the announcement of Dolly's birth until he registered a patent. And other observers speculated about the implications of patenting clones for perceptions of the person. Is the body to become little more than a commodity, a commercial entity that can be simply constructed as a product?

Just as the GWU experiment evoked images of a cloning industry and breeding factories, so Dolly evoked cynical references to "test-tube capitalists," and sardonic queries about a market for genetic "factory seconds" and "irregulars." A World Wide Web site called Dreamtech satirized the issues by advertising a commercial service to create either "custom clones" or "designer clones." The "company" would clone various celebrities for a range of licensing fees, depending on the anticipated value of the product. The advertisement also offered a personal extraction kit, surrogate services, rapid delivery, and a backup embryo. . . .

Calls for Regulation of Cloning

The messages evoked by Dolly have ranged from promises of progress to portents of peril, from images of miracles to visions of apocalypse. There were many calls for regulation and for a moratorium on cloning experiments. Just a week after the cloning of Dolly, President [Bill] Clinton issued a directive banning the use of federal funds to support research on the cloning of human beings. So too, the president of France, the president of the European Commission, the director-general of Unesco, and the Vatican all called for a moratorium on research on cloning, which had clearly become politically unacceptable.

As political and social pressures grew, scientists responded, defending the importance of the work. Media images were "selling science short." The calls for regulations and restrictions, they argued, ignored the medical benefits that could follow from cloning experiments and their potential contribution to the development of life-saving treatments, skin grafts for burn victims, treatments for infertile couples, and a means of testing new drugs. We are not interested in playing God, said James Geraghty, president of the biotechnology firm Genzyme, but in "playing doctor." Mammalian cloning could help to generate tissue for organ transplantation and encourage transgenics experimentation. And certainly research using cloning would enhance scientific knowledge about cell differentiation. The politicians who sought a ban on cloning research, said scientists, were "shooting from the hip." Science fiction, they insisted, should not be the guide to science policy.

Responding to the growing threat of regulation, a group of prominent scholars from the International Academy of Humanism signed a "Defense of Cloning and the Integrity of Research." This academy, a group of self-identified "secular humanists," have, since the debates over teaching creation theory in the schools during the 1970s, been inclined to interpret every critique of science and every discussion about regulation as a manifestation of antiscience sentiment. There were, they claimed, no particularly profound moral issues related to cloning, but only a "Luddite rejection" of cloning by "advocates of supernatural and spiritual agendas." They included in this Luddite [antitechnology] group the President's National Bioethics Advisory Commission, which was convened in 1997 to consider moral issues and to recommend government policy.

This 18-member commission had focused on potential physical and psychological risks as well as the moral acceptability of cloning. After three months of intensive deliberation, it concluded that the government should continue its moratorium on federal funding for cloning research. . . . President Clinton accepted the report and sent legislative recommendations to Congress. In a speech in the Rose Garden, he said: "Cloning has the potential to threaten the sacred family bonds at the core of our ideals and our society . . . to make our children objects rather than cherished individuals." But the very same day, a Switzerland-based group, supported by a group of investors, launched an international company called Valiant Ventures Ltd. It claims to provide a "Clonaid" service for wealthy parents worldwide who want to have a child cloned. The cost would be just $200,000. In addition, the company would provide safe storage of the tissue from any "beloved person" so that it could be cloned at a later date in case of death. This company also offered to support the efforts of Dr. Richard Seed, the physicist who said, in 1998, that he intended to open a commercial clinic to clone people.

Dolly Has Become a Symbol

Dolly, after all, [was] only a sheep, and she is depicted again and again as cuddly and cute. But as a symbolic site for the exploration of identity, heredity, destiny, and the social meaning of science, she is a spectacular beast. She is a compelling actor in contemporary dreams about science—evoking for some euphoric fantasies; for others horrible nightmares and the fear of science out of control. She offers up the possibility of hyperrationality in the management of bodies and of complete genetic control of cows, sheep, and humans as well. She offers the specter of technical decisions that will turn all bodies (human and animal) into intentional products, manufactured and designed "on purpose." She evokes a way of thinking about bodies as little more than efficient mechanisms for the production of "value"—be it milk, or meat, or creative imagination. But she is also a focus of popular mistrust of research that is tied to commercial interests.

Dolly can thus be regarded less as a sheep than as a microcosm of the history of science—a symbol of the rich interconnections between animals and human beings, of the struggles between technological changes and moral tenets, of the tensions between the advance of scientific knowledge and demands for political expediency in the face of public concerns.

Popular speculations about science and its terrors have often been dismissed as based on journalistic ignorance of science, sensationalism, or willful misinterpretation for the sake of making news. But media messages matter, and often reflect legitimate concerns. Widely disseminated images and narratives have real effects, regardless of their relationship to the technical details of the scientific work. They shape the way people think about new technologies, assess their impacts, and develop ways to control them.

The popular responses to Dolly are especially important because they convey meanings that extend well beyond the single experiment. Dolly has become far more than a biological entity; she is a cultural icon, a symbol, a way to define the meaning of personhood and to express concerns about the forces shaping our lives. She provides a window on popular beliefs about human nature and the social order, on public fears of science and its power in society, and on concerns about the human future in the biotechnology age. She is a stunning image in the popular imagination.

Common Beliefs About Human Cloning Are Myths

Gregory E. Pence

Gregory E. Pence is a professor in the philosophy department and School of Medicine at the University of Alabama. He is the author of several books and many articles about genetic engineering and bioethics, and he has testified about cloning before congressional committees. In the following selection, he discusses what he believes are the top ten myths concerning human cloning. Although experts attest that all of these ideas are false, Pence highlights the controversies that surround them. He argues that because of the pervasiveness of these myths, even the word cloning *has acquired unpleasant connotations among the general public. Pence believes that it is not possible to have a fair discussion using this word and that perhaps other terms should be substituted. He suggests, for example, that someone created by cloning should not be called a "clone," but should be referred to simply as a person.*

[Many of the ideas people have about human cloning are untrue. Here are the top ten myths.]

1. Cloning Xeroxes a person.

Cloning merely re-creates the genes of the ancestor, not what he has learned or experienced. Technically, it re-creates the genotype, not the phenotype. (Even at that, only 99% of those genes get re-created because 1% of such a child's genes would come from those in the egg—mitochondrial DNA.) Conventional wisdom holds that about half of who we are comes from our genes, the other half, from the environment.

Cloning cannot re-create what in us came from the environment; it also cannot re-create memories. The false belief

Gregory E. Pence, "The Top Ten Myths About Human Cloning," www.human cloning.org, 2001. Copyright © 2001 by Gregory E. Pence. Reproduced by permission.

that cloning re-creates a person stems in part from the common, current false belief in simplistic, genetic reductionism, i.e., that a person really is just determined by his genes. No reputable geneticist or psychologist believes this.

2. Human cloning is replication or making children into commodities.

Opponents of cloning often use these words to beg the question, to assume that children created by parents by a new method would not be loved. Similar things were said about "test tube" babies, who turned out to be some of the most-wanted, most-loved babies ever created in human history.

Indeed, the opposite is true: evolution has created us with sex drives such that, if we do not carefully use contraception, children occur. Because children get created this way without being wanted, sexual reproduction is more likely to create unwanted, and hence possibly unloved, children than human cloning.

Lawyers opposing cloning have a special reason for using these pejorative words. If cloning is just a new form of human reproduction, then it is constitutionally protected from interference by the state. Several Supreme Court decisions declare that all forms of human reproduction, including the right not to reproduce, cannot be abridged by government.

Use of words such as "replication" and "commodification" also assumes artificial wombs or commercial motives; about these fallacies, see below.

3. Human cloning reduces biological diversity.

Population genetics says otherwise. Six billion people now exist, soon to be eight billion, and most of them reproduce. Cloning requires in vitro [outside the body] fertilization, which is expensive and inefficient, with only a 20% success rate. Since 1978, at most a half million babies have been produced this way, or at most, one out of 12,000 babies.

Over decades and with such great numbers, populations follow the Law of Regression to the Mean [a statistical principle dealing with the way things tend to return to normal]. This means that, even if someone tried to create a superior race by cloning, it would fail, because cloned people would have children with non-cloned people, and resulting genetic hybrids would soon be normalized.

Cloning is simply a tool. It could be used with the motive of creating uniformity (but would fail, because of above), or it could be used for the opposite reason, to try to increase diversity (which would also fail, for the same reason).

4. People created by cloning would be less ensouled than normal humans, or would be sub-human.

A human who had the same number of chromosomes as a child created sexually, who was gestated by a woman, and who talked, felt, and spoke as any other human, would ethically be human and a person. It is by now a principle of ethics that the origins of a person, be it from mixed-race parents, unmarried parents, in vitro fertilization, or a gay male couple hiring a surrogate mother, do not affect the personhood of the child born. The same would be true of a child created by cloning (who, of course, has to be gestated for nine months by a woman).

Every deviation from normal reproduction has always been faced with this fear. Children greeted by sperm donation, in vitro fertilization, and surrogate motherhood were predicted to be less-than-human, but were not.

A variation predicts that while, in fact, they will not be less-than-human, people will treat them this way and hence, such children will be harmed. This objection reifies prejudice and makes it an ethical justification, which it is wrong to do. The correct response to prejudice is to expose it for what it is, combat it with reason and with evidence not validate it as an ethical reason.

5. People created by cloning could be used for spare organs for normal humans.

Nothing could be done to a person created by cloning that right now could not be done to your brother or to a person's twin. The U.S. Constitution strongly implies that once a human fetus is outside the womb and alive, he has rights. Decisions backing this up give him rights to inherit property, rights not to suffer discrimination because of disability, and rights to U.S. citizenship.

A variation of this myth assumes that a dictator could make cloned humans into special SWAT teams or suicidal bombers. But nothing about originating people this way gives anyone any special power over the resulting humans, who would have free will. Besides, if a dictator wants to create such assassins, he need not wait for cloning but can take orphans and try to indoctrinate them now in isolated camps.

6. All people created from the same genotype would be raised in batches and share secret empathy or communication.

Pure science fiction. If I wanted to re-create the genotype of my funny Uncle Harry, why would my wife want to gestate 5 or 6 other babies at the same time? Indeed, we now know that the womb cannot support more than 2–3 fetuses without creating a likely disability in one. Guidelines now call for no more than two embryos to be introduced by in vitro fertilization, which of course is required to use cloning.

Such assumptions about cloned humans being created in batches are linked to nightmarish science fiction scenarios where humane society has been destroyed and where industrialized machines have taken over human reproduction. But this is just someone's nightmare, not facts upon which to base state and federal laws.

7. Scientists who work on human cloning are evil or motivated by bad motives.

The stuff of Hollywood and scary writers. Scientists are just people. Most of them have kids of their own and care a lot for kids. No one wants to bring a handicapped child into the world. Movies and novels never portray life scientists with sympathy. This anti-science prejudice started with Mary Shelley's Frankenstein and continues with nefarious scientists working for the Government on *The X Files*.

People who call themselves scientists and grandstand for television, such as Richard Seed and Brigette Boisselier of the Raelians, are not real scientists but people who use the aura of science to gain attention. Real scientists don't spend all their time flying around the world to be on TV but stay at home in their clinics doing their work.

8. Babies created by cloning could be grown in artificial wombs.

Nope, sorry. Medicine has been trying for fifty years to create an artificial womb, but has never come close to succeeding. Indeed, controversial experiments in 1973 on live-born fetuses in studying artificial wombs effectively shut down such research.

Finally, if anything like such wombs existed, we could save premature babies, who haven't developed lung function, but unfortunately, we still can't—premature babies who can't breathe at all die. Thus, any human baby still needs a human woman to gestate him for at least six months, and to be healthy, nine months. This puts the lie to many science fiction stories and to many predictions about cloning and industrial reproduction.

9. Only selfish people want to create a child by cloning.

First, this assumes that ordinary people don't create children for selfish reasons, such as a desire to have someone take care of them in old age, a desire to see part of themselves continue after death, and/or the desire to leave their estate to someone. Many people are hypocritical or deceived about why they came to have children. Very few people just decide that they want to bring more joy into the world, and hence create a child to raise and support for life as an end-in-himself. Let's be honest here. Second, a couple using cloning need not create a copy of one of them. As said above, Uncle Harry could be a prime candidate.

On the other hand, if a couple chooses a famous person, critics accuse them of creating designer babies. Either way, they can't win: if they re-create one of their genotypes, they are narcissistic; if they choose someone else's genes, they're guilty of creating designer babies.

In general, why should a couple using cloning have a higher justification required of them than a couple using sexual reproduction? If we ask: what counts as a good reason for creating a child, then why should cloning have any special test that is not required for sexual reproduction? Indeed, and more generally, what right does government have to require, or judge, any couple's reasons for having a child, even if they are seen by others to be selfish?

Couples desiring to use cloning should not bear an undue burden of justification.

10. Human cloning is inherently evil: it can only be used for bad purposes by bad people.

No, it's just a tool, just another way to create a family. A long legacy in science fiction novels and movies make the word "cloning" so fraught with bad connotations that it can hardly be used in any discussion that purports to be impartial. It is like discussing equal rights for women by starting to discuss whether "the chicks" would fare better with equal rights. To most people, "cloning" implies selfish parents, crazy scientists, and out-of-control technology, so a fair discussion using this word isn't possible. Perhaps the phrase, "somatic cell nuclear transplantation" is better, even if it's a scientific mouthful. So if we shouldn't call a person created by cloning, a "clone," what should we call him? Answer: a person.

Human Reproductive Cloning Should Be Banned, but Therapeutic Cloning Should Be Allowed

Gerald Ford

Gerald Ford was the thirty-eighth president of the United States. He served in office from 1974 to 1977 and is presently retired. In the following selection, he argues that although reproductive cloning would be, in his opinion, "a perversion of science," therapeutic cloning should be allowed. He believes that many Americans suffering from chronic or debilitating diseases might be cured by therapeutic cloning, and that they deserve the best medical treatments science can develop. At the time President Ford wrote this article, a bill banning both types of cloning was before Congress, and he presents his reasons for opposing it. That bill did not pass.

It is a troubling paradox of American politics: All too often the issues that most cry out for thoughtful, dispassionate consideration are reduced to sound bites. Further distorted in the name of ideology or partisanship, they can become oversimplified to the point of caricature. The public—and public policy—suffer, if only because there are some phrases virtually guaranteed to polarize any debate before it gets started.

Affirmative action. Reproductive rights. Gay rights. Now you can add cloning to the list. For many, the word conjures up sinister images of mad scientists laying claim to God-like powers. From there it is a short step toward a soulless state, wherein assembly-line man is robbed of his individuality by science run amok. It's hard to imagine a more frightening scenario.

But is it real? Growing up in Grand Rapids, Mich., I was taught to put my faith in God, not government, and never to confuse the two. On the verge of my 89th birthday, I am not likely to change this view.

That's why I share the concerns of many about reproductive cloning, which in theory, at least, could lead to Dr. Frankenstein's vision of laboratory-manufactured humans. To me this is a perversion of science. Legislation has been introduced that would outlaw the cloning of human beings.

At the same time, this legislation would allow continued research into therapeutic cloning—more precisely known as somatic cell nuclear transfer, or nuclear transportation—a very different branch of science that holds limitless potential to improve or extend life for 130 million Americans now suffering from some chronic or debilitating condition.

The anguish of these people is multiplied by the number of family members struggling to care for victims of heart disease, diabetes, Alzheimer's and Parkinson's, spinal cord injury and a vast array of other ailments. For every Ronald Reagan [who suffered from Alzheimer's disease], cruelly deprived of the knowledge of his pivotal place in our history, there are millions of elderly, and not so elderly, citizens who will never get their names in the history books, although they are similarly imprisoned in memory's darkened rooms. They deserve more than our sympathy. They deserve the finest treatment imaginable by the world's best scientists.

Banning Therapeutic Cloning Would Be Harmful

Unfortunately, they may not get it. In stark contrast to the Human Cloning Prohibition Act sponsored by Sens. Arlen Specter, Dianne Feinstein, Orrin Hatch and Edward M. Kennedy, other members of Congress in both houses are [as of 2002] trying to legislate an absolute ban on all cloning, therapeutic as well as reproductive.

Under terms of the Brownback-Landrieu bill in the Senate, and its House counterpart, H.R. 2505, promising regenerative therapies would be criminalized. This is not locking the lid on Pandora's box. It is slamming the door to lifesaving cures and treatments merely because they are new.

No fewer than 40 Nobel laureates have warned that such legislation "would foreclose the legitimate use of nuclear transplantation . . . and impede progress against some of the most debilitating diseases known to man."

Nor would it end there. Long in the vanguard of scientific discovery, American scientists and public policymakers have done much to shape sound scientific policies throughout the world. To walk away from the advances already achieved through therapeutic cloning is to surrender this leadership. It is to turn our back on the worldwide debate over harnessing, controlling and sharing these powerful new discoveries. It is to reject much of our history and still more of our future.

This is not an either/or question. It is a false choice that says we can have medical breakthroughs or we can safeguard human individuality—but we can't do both. No one knows this better than the scientific researcher. The frontiers of knowledge are often lonely and sometimes uncivilized. Government has a mandate to police these regions and to guard against unethical or exploitative conduct, without suffocating the instinct for exploration and self-improvement that defines the human race.

Notwithstanding the efforts of some scientists, men are not to be confused with sheep. So what is it that sets us apart? Among other things, it is our capacity for faith—complemented by our God-given curiosity, our dissatisfaction with limits and our stubborn refusal to acquiesce in early death or to suffer passively through debilitating illnesses thinly disguised as life.

Fortunately, we have recent precedent to help guide us through the forest of scientific and political uncertainty. During my presidency, similar questions were raised about research into recombinant DNA. After careful deliberation, safeguards were devised to ensure that this promising new line of inquiry would be closely monitored. It was a measured response to a sensitive issue, and it has resulted in advances that were unimaginable in the 1970s.

A quarter-century later, would anyone turn back the clock? Would anyone discard vaccines traceable to recombinant DNA research? Would they dismiss the promising new strategies to prevent or combat AIDS, diabetes and cancer?

Bills have already been put forward that ban human [reproductive] cloning and provide stiff penalties for it, while allowing continued research into the promise of nuclear transfer research. I call on Congress to pick up the mantle of leadership on this important issue and craft a compromise solution that works.

Both Human Reproductive Cloning and Therapeutic Cloning Should Be Banned

George W. Bush

George W. Bush is the forty-third president of the United States. In the following speech, which he gave at the White House in 2002 and which was televised, he argued in favor of a bill then before Congress that would have banned all human cloning. President Bush gave four reasons why he believes there should be such a ban. First, in his opinion, all human cloning would be unethical because it would involve the exploitation or destruction of human life. Second, it would be impossible to enforce a ban against reproductive cloning if research cloning was permitted. Third, there is no evidence that therapeutic cloning would really provide cures for disease. And fourth, if it did offer cures, that would create a market for egg donors, which he feels would lead to exploitation of women. President Bush stated that the bill to ban cloning had wide support across the political spectrum. However, when Congress later voted on it, it did not pass.

Well, thank you all so very much for coming to the White House. It's my honor to welcome you to the people's house.

I particularly want to honor three folks who I had the honor of meeting earlier: Joni Tada, Jim Kelly and Steve Mc-Donald [paralyzed persons who oppose therapeutic cloning]. I want to thank you for your courage, I want to thank you for your wisdom, I want to thank you for your extraordinary perseverence and faith. They have triumphed in the face of physical disability and share a deep commitment to medicine that is practiced ethically and humanely.

George W. Bush, "President Bush Calls on Senate to Back Human Cloning Ban," www.whitehouse.gov, April 10, 2002.

All of us here today believe in the promise of modern medicine. We're hopeful about where science may take us. And we're also here because we believe in the principles of ethical medicine.

As we seek to improve human life, we must always preserve human dignity. And therefore, we must prevent human cloning by stopping it before it starts. . . .

We live in a time of tremendous medical progress. [In 2001], scientists first cracked the human genetic code—one of the most important advances in scientific history. Already, scientists are developing new diagnostic tools so that each of us can know our risk of disease and act to prevent them.

One day soon, precise therapies will be custom made for our own genetic makeup. We're on the threshold of historic breakthroughs against AIDS and Alzheimer's Disease and cancer and diabetes and heart disease and Parkinson's Disease. And that's incredibly positive.

Medical Research Must Be Ethical

Our age may be known to history as the age of genetic medicine, a time when many of the most feared illnesses were overcome.

Our age must also be defined by the care and restraint and responsibility with which we take up these new scientific powers.

Advances in biomedical technology must never come at the expense of human conscience. As we seek what is possible, we must always ask what is right, and we must not forget that even the most noble ends do not justify any means.

Science has set before us decisions of immense consequence. We can pursue medical research with a clear sense of moral purpose or we can travel without an ethical compass into a world we could live to regret. Science now presses forward the issue of human cloning. How we answer the question of human cloning will place us on one path or the other.

Human cloning is the laboratory production of individuals who are genetically identical to another human being. Cloning is achieved by putting the genetic material from a donor into a woman's egg, which has had its nucleus removed. As a result, the new or cloned embryo is an identical copy of only the donor. Human cloning has moved from science fiction into science.

One biotech company [Advanced Cell Technology of Worcester, MA] has already began producing embryonic human clones for research purposes. Chinese scientists have derived stem cells from cloned embryos created by combining human DNA and rabbit eggs. Others have announced plans to produce cloned children, despite the fact that laboratory cloning of animals has led to spontaneous abortions and terrible, terrible abnormalities.

Human cloning is deeply troubling to me, and to most Americans. Life is a creation, not a commodity. Our children are gifts to be loved and protected, not products to be designed and manufactured. Allowing cloning would be taking a significant step toward a society in which human beings are grown for spare body parts, and children are engineered to custom specifications; and that's not acceptable.

In the current debate over human cloning, two terms are being used: reproductive cloning and research [therapeutic] cloning. Reproductive cloning involves creating a cloned embryo and implanting it into a woman with the goal of creating a child. Fortunately, nearly every American agrees that this practice should be banned. Research cloning, on the other hand, involves the creation of cloned human embryos which are then destroyed to derive stem cells.

All Human Cloning Is Wrong

I believe all human cloning is wrong, and both forms of cloning ought to be banned, for the following reasons. First, anything other than a total ban on human cloning would be unethical. Research cloning would contradict the most fundamental principle of medical ethics, that no human life should be exploited or extinguished for the benefit of another.

Yet a law permitting research cloning, while forbidding the birth of a cloned child, would require the destruction of nascent human life. Secondly, anything other than a total ban on human cloning would be virtually impossible to enforce. Cloned human embryos created for research would be widely available in laboratories and embryo farms. Once cloned embryos were available, implantation would take place. Even the tightest regulations and strict policing would not prevent or detect the birth of cloned babies.

Third, the benefits of research cloning are highly speculative. Advocates of research cloning argue that stem cells obtained from cloned embryos would be injected into a genetically identical individual without risk of tissue rejection. But there is evidence, based on animal studies, that cells derived from cloned embryos may indeed be rejected.

Yet even if research cloning were medically effective, every person who wanted to benefit would need an embryonic clone of his or her own, to provide the designer tissues. This would create a massive national market for eggs and egg donors, and exploitation of women's bodies that we cannot and must not allow.

Other Forms of Biotechnology Are Promising

I stand firm in my opposition to human cloning. And at the same time, we will pursue other promising and ethical ways to relieve suffering through biotechnology. This year for the first time, federal dollars will go towards supporting human embryonic stem cell research consistent with the ethical guidelines I announced [in] August [2001].

The National Institutes of Health [NIH] is also funding a broad range of animal and human adult stem cell research.

Adult stem cells which do not require the destruction of human embryos and which yield tissues which can be transplanted without rejection are more versatile that originally thought.

We're making progress. We're learning more about them. And therapies developed from adult stem cells are already helping suffering people.

I support increasing the research budget of the NIH, and I ask Congress to join me in that support. And at the same time, I strongly support a comprehensive law against all human cloning. And I endorse the bill—wholeheartedly endorse the bill—sponsored by Senator Brownback [R-KS] and Senator Mary Landrieu [D-LA].

This carefully drafted bill would ban all human cloning in the United States, including the cloning of embryos for research. It is nearly identical to the bipartisan legislation that last year passed the House of Representatives by more than a 100-vote margin. It has wide support across the political spectrum, liberals and conservatives support it, religious people and nonreligious people support it. Those who are pro-choice and those who are pro-life support the bill.

This is a diverse coalition, united by a commitment to prevent the cloning and exploitation of human beings. It would be a mistake for the United States Senate to allow any kind of human cloning to come out of that chamber.

I'm an incurable optimist about the future of our country. I know we can achieve great things. We can make the world more peaceful, we can become a more compassionate nation. We can push the limits of medical science. I truly believe that we're going to bring hope and healing to countless lives across the country. And as we do, I will insist that we always maintain the highest of ethical standards.

Thank you all for coming. God bless.

Religious Views of Cloning Do Not Agree

Bob Sullivan

Bob Sullivan is a technology consultant for MSNBC, an Internet news service. He is the winner of the prestigious 2002 Society of Professional Journalists Public Service Award. In the following selection he explains the views of the major religions toward cloning. Members of these religions do not agree among themselves as to whether human cloning is wrong or not, Sullivan notes. People opposed to therapeutic cloning believe that destruction of a human embryo during research is murder; but, as Sullivan writes, most Jews do not believe that, nor do they believe cloning is "playing God." Catholics and conservative Christians generally oppose all human cloning. Views among other Christians—as well as among Buddhists, Hindus, and Muslims—are diverse, and some have no religious objection even to reproductive cloning. As Sullivan reports, a 2004 survey has shown that the majority of Americans base their attitude toward cloning on their individual opinions rather than on religious dogma.

The debate over whether scientists are "playing God" has probably never been more real than now, as humans consider calling forth the spark of life, seemingly without divine intervention. However, a confused population looking for clear ethical wisdom on cloning might be disappointed: Beyond issuing a general call for caution, the world's spiritual leaders hardly speak with one voice on the cloning debate.

What would Jesus do? Or Buddha? Or the Dalai Lama? The announcement of sheep-clone Dolly in 1997 sent many religious leaders to the pulpit. Others scrambled through religious texts looking for guidance. There were plenty of swift condemnations.

Bob Sullivan, "Religions Reveal Little Consensus on Cloning," MSNBC.com, 2005.
Copyright © 2005 by Bob Sullivan. Reproduced by permission.

But as the realities and limitations of science have removed some of the haze surrounding cloning, the philosophical and religious debates have also come into focus.

Today, conservative Christians are still unmoved from their blanket opposition to all cloning. Other faiths have found room in their traditions for therapeutic cloning—the use of cloned cells for research and health reasons, but not for breeding humans. Some even find ethical room for the cloning of humans.

But in almost every case, the religious debate is still open-ended. Other than opposition to the more sinister possibilities, such as the creation of "spare-parts" humans, there is hardly consensus about the ethics of cloning. In the absence of a central teaching authority, akin to the Roman Catholic Church's Congregation for the Doctrine of the Faith, many religious scholars are still openly debating the pros and cons of a powerful new science that could bring as much potential for hope as for horror.

Three Basic Questions

The discussion eventually wraps itself around three central questions: Would cloning somehow corrupt traditional family relationships and lineage? Is destruction of a fertilized embryo during research murder? And perhaps more fundamentally, does cloning meddle with God's universe in a way that humans shouldn't?

Picking a position on cloning is actually an exercise in revisiting basic religious beliefs, says Courtney Campbell, director of the Program for Ethics, Science and the Environment at Oregon State University.

For example, most Jews and Muslims don't consider a fertilized embryo to have full human status, which essentially gives a green light to therapeutic cloning research. In that sense, the discussion about therapeutic cloning tends to follow lines similar to the debate over stem cell research and, ultimately, abortion.

"Thinking about cloning ought to require traditions to go back and think through basic tenets, such as does life really begin at conception," Campbell said. "You can't avoid that question."

To most faithful, answering such deep questions requires study of religious texts. Some people might think thousand-year-old writings would offer little guidance on 21st-century scientific morality, but that's not true, says Rabbi Edward Reichman, assistant professor of philosophy and history at Yeshiva University Einstein College of Medicine.

"The (Jewish) law is relevant to any imaginable technology," he said. "When you apply the law to a new technology, you can seek direct precedent, or you can . . . seek to distill a principle of the law that applies.

"With evolution, Darwin, Copernicus, it was fundamentally the same. It was an unknown thing one couldn't have dreamed of when the law was written, but where the principles applied."

Jewish law is squarely on the side of medical research that has potential to save and preserve life, Reichman said. As a result, Jewish scholars are generally among the most vocal religious leaders in support of therapeutic cloning.

"The Jewish faith generally welcomes new technologies and sciences in as much as they can benefit the world, especially medicine. We do not necessarily perceive all advances as stepping on God's toes," he said.

Christian Views Are Diverse

But that's exactly the interpretation arrived at by Roman Catholic scholars after examining the Bible and Canon Law. Back in 1987, the church became the leading voice against human cloning of any kind. In a document called "Donum Vitae," Roman Catholics were told that cloning was "considered contrary to the moral law, since (it is in) opposition to the dignity both of human procreation and of the conjugal union."

The church still holds that position, which is also supported by conservative Christians such as Southern Baptists. However, there is great diversity of opinion among other Christian denominations, and even within those denominations.

Oregon State's Campbell compiled the most comprehensive look at religious perspectives in 1997, for the National Bioethics Advisory Commission appointed by then-President Bill Clinton.

Campbell used a simple traffic-light system to classify the religious points of view: Catholics and Southern Baptists issue clear red lights on both therapeutic and human cloning. But among "mainline" Protestants such as the Lutheran and Episcopal faiths, Campbell found some green and yellow lights.

"Some traditions and leading figures in conservative Protestantism who were opposed to human cloning for reproductive reasons have come to see that given the ambiguity about their own views about the status of embryonic life, and given the potential for health benefits, they could be opposed to reproductive cloning, but affirm therapeutic cloning," Campbell said. The main reason, Campbell says, is the tradition of emphasizing individual choice over central dogma.

Buddhism: Yes and No

Some other faiths are even harder to pin down. For example, there is no stated position among Buddhists on cloning, so scholars like Campbell are left only to interpret the tradition's precepts on their own.

Buddhism might be willing to accept cloning, Campbell said, because it represents a leap in modern science and self-understanding that could be considered a path to enlightenment. On the other hand, the Eightfold Path prohibits harm to any sentient beings, which could be seen in the destruction of cells necessary to perform cloning research. Campbell's judgment: a yellow light on the issues raised by human cloning, and a flashing red light on other implications of cloning research.

Damien Keown, professor at Goldsmiths College in London and perhaps the best-known expert on possible Buddhist responses to cloning, generally agreed. He said the tradition doesn't have the same kind of fundamental moral opposition that can be found in Christian faiths. Buddhists already believe in non-sexual reproduction, for example, since Buddhism teaches that life can come into being through supernatural phenomenon like spontaneous generation. "Life can thus legitimately begin in more ways than one," he said.

"For Christians, to bring into being a new human or animal life by cloning as opposed to normal sexual reproduction is to 'play God' and usurp the power of the creator. This is not a problem for Buddhism, because in Buddhism the creation of new life is not seen as a 'gift from God,'" Keown said in a recent paper. "For this reason the technique in itself would not be seen as problematic."

Buddhism sees human individuality as a mirage, so adherents wouldn't share some of the other philosophical complaints that Western thinkers have about cloning, as it pertains to devaluing an individual's personality or character by creating copies.

But that hardly means Buddhists will welcome clones. On more practical grounds, Buddhism promotes ultimate respect to every sentient being, and that generally includes cells born out of research. Destroying such cells, even in research on animal cloning, runs contrary to Buddhist teaching.

"It is hard to see what purposes—scientific or otherwise—can justify the dehumanization that results when life is created and manipulated for other ends," Keown said. "We should not forget that Ian Wilmut, the creator of Dolly [the cloned sheep], failed 276 times before Dolly was conceived."

Hindu and Muslim Views Vary

Hindu religious scholars have issued flashing red lights, according to Campbell—which means they are calling for a temporary pause to provide time to think, but have not issued an outright objection of human cloning.

A Hindu's sense of the world and the relationship between people and Creator is very different from Western traditions, so Hindus also wouldn't have the same fundamental objection to "playing God" that Christians might. But there are plenty of concerns about the desire for greed and power that might be served by aggressive scientists who call for cloning.

Diversity among Muslims makes an authoritative description of Islamic thought on cloning nearly impossible. Dr. Abdulaziz Sachedina, University of Virginia professor and a leading U.S. scholar on Muslim thought regarding cloning, believes that most Muslims will eventually agree that scientists wouldn't have discovered cloning if Allah hadn't willed it. So cloning for the purpose of enhancing the chances of procreating within a solid family structure will be "regarded as an act of faith in the ultimate will of God as the Giver of all life."

But he's hardly without opponents. Nasser Farid Wasel, Egypt's Mufti, said in 1999 that cloning clearly contradicts Islam. Other muftis have gone further, saying scientists who clone are doing Satan's work.

Dr. Ibrahim B. Syed, director of the Islamic Research Foundation International and an outspoken cloning supporter, says such absolute statements from religious leaders only serve to complicate the conversation.

"Anything new, just as a reaction, they oppose it," Syed said. "Our religious leaders have little knowledge of evolving technologies." But the problem works both ways, he conceded.

"The scientists don't know anything about religious beliefs, often."

Science vs. Religion

Scientific advances have shaken religious beliefs to their roots repeatedly through the ages. Charles Darwin did it. Copernicus did it. And now, companies like Advanced Cell Technologies are doing it.

But as much as religious leaders want to push scientists to think more about the morality of their work, scientists are pushing religious leaders back to the basic tenets of their faiths, where they scramble to make sense of a world teetering on the razor's edge of irreversible change.

While it might be a frightening moment, it's also a grand opportunity, Campbell said.

"Science can be a spur to creative and innovative theological thought," he said. "And I think what is a crying need is for the church to be a forum for discussion with engaged dialogue between science and religion, and be a venue for civic conversation."

In the debate over cloning, will religious views ultimately matter? Already, some scientists are working faster than ethicists on cloning. And at least in the United States, there is an open question about the weight given to religious leaders' opinions on cloning.

Four out of five people said they opposed cloning in a survey conducted [in 2004] for the Pew Forum on Religion and Public Life and the Pew Research Center for the People and the Press. But only one in four Catholics and one in three Protestants cited religious beliefs as the main reasons for their opposition. Pollsters say many Americans pride themselves on developing their own opinions rather than consulting religious dogma—which means that the key decisions on cloning are much more likely to be made in the House of Representatives than in a house of God.

The Cloning of Animals

Cloning May Have Limited Applications in Livestock Farming

Suzanne Quick

Suzanne Quick is a science reporter for the Milwaukee Journal Sentinel. *In the following selection she discusses the cloning of farm animals. A sheep, Dolly, was the first mammal cloned because it was expected that cloning might revolutionize agriculture. However, the U.S. Food and Drug Administration [FDA] has delayed making a decision about the safety of products obtained from cloned animals and has asked livestock producers not to put them into the food chain. This has been a disappointment to farmers, and, as Quick reports, many have begun to question whether cloning will ever be useful for the production of food.*

In the world of biotech and biomedicine, it's usually the mouse or primate that takes center stage. But when the first cloned animal from adult cells was announced, the spotlight fell on a fleecy-white Scottish sheep named Dolly.

Dolly was chosen because of the potential she and other large farm animals had for revolutionizing agriculture and medicine.

But [in 2005] nearly a decade after her birth—and 18 years since Neal First, a retired University of Wisconsin–Madison researcher, first cloned calves from embryonic cells—cloned animals have yet to make it to the shelf of any American supermarket or pharmacy.

The U.S. Food and Drug Administration has asked livestock producers to refrain from putting animal clones and their progeny into the food chain. And the FDA is in discussions with other federal agencies about how best to verify the safety of these products.

This has come as a disappointment for scientists and farmers who foresaw herds of sheep fleeced in the finest of wools, dairy cows with the ability to pump out tens of gallons of milk every day and giant porkers belted with bellies of bacon.

While most researchers agree that the potential for medical advances using cloned livestock remains, many have begun to question how cloning could advance animal husbandry. The benefits, they say, are limited to basic research, conservation of rare breeds, creation of only female chickens to lay eggs and the possibility of disease resistance. Dreams of superior flocks roaming the agricultural hinterlands are misguided and farfetched, they say.

"We're just too good at it," said Bruce Whitelaw, a researcher at the Roslin Institute in Scotland, referring to conventional farming. Cloning and transgenics—adding or deleting genes in an animal—will add little, if anything, to advances already made in livestock agriculture since World War II, he said.

"I mean, food is cheap," he said. And these new technologies—as unwieldy and expensive as they are—will only add cost.

That makes agricultural companies and government agencies reluctant to funnel money into cloning. The lack of monetary support, say researchers, has slowed the technology, making it more unlikely that it'll ever reach the consumer's shelf.

First believes that if products from cloned animals were tastier and cheaper than those from conventionally bred animals, a market would develop.

"We thought nobody would buy milk" from cows that had been given growth hormones, he said. But the U.S. Department of Agriculture slapped stickers on milk cartons to warn consumers, and few balked.

Misconceptions and Uncertainty

John Woolliams, a geneticist at the Roslin Institute, said more fundamental concerns about large-scale livestock cloning must be considered. He believes that entire herds composed of the same superior cow just don't make sense.

First of all, he said, the idea that "somehow the perfect cow exists" is nonsense. Even if it did, he said, a herd made up of genetically identical animals would increase the likelihood of inbreeding, as well as make the animals more vulnerable to disease.

But that's not all. A common misconception exists that if farmers could clone their best animals, they would somehow reach the apex of livestock production, he said. ABS Global of DeForest, Wis., was a leader in the late 1990s in trying to create ways of mass producing clones.

Unfortunately, said Woolliams, that's not the way it works.

Current breeding schemes, which include conventionally bred animals, try to increase production by 1% to 5%. Meaning, a dairy farmer expects his cows to produce slightly more milk with each new generation.

With a clone, that improvement would cease.

"Cloning is a brick wall for progress," Woolliams said.

Added to that, say others, is the uncertainty about what role genes and the environment play on an animal's productivity.

"Let's say you clone an animal that has incredible success at reproducing," said Robert Collier, a professor of animal studies at the University of Arizona in Tucson. "Maybe it produced 70,000 offspring in its lifetime, and you want to preserve that success by cloning it. OK. You clone it. Now you send 1,000 of its clones to 1,000 different farms around the

United States. Most of those clones are not going to have the same reproductive success."

That's because "each farm will have a different set of environmental factors. And the environment is going to affect a cow's ability to reproduce," he said.

Modest Possibilities

But here is where cloning may prove to be a scientific boon. Researchers and farmers could learn from clones how an animal's environment and genes affect its productivity, temperament and health.

We have "very little understanding about genetic diversity and the way it buffers disease," Woolliams said. Cloning would allow researchers to learn more about this area of livestock management and possibly enable them to make animals more resistant to disease.

Lou Hawthorne, CEO for Genetics Savings & Clone Inc., a pet-cloning outfit . . . , said cloning will provide scientists with "the grand experiment of nature versus nurture."

Woolliams and others believe cloning may have other modest impacts.

"I don't think many people realize it," but 50% of all baby chickens are killed every year, said Jim McWhir, a geneticist and developmental biologist at the Roslin Institute.

The female is desired in egg-laying breeds; the male is desired in meat breeds. The gender not wanted at a specific farm is killed.

If farmers could be assured that all chicks born on their farms were the same sex, which they could by cloning them, it would save money, chicken lives and the time it takes to handle each chick to determine its sex, said Ron Kean, a UW [University of Wisconsin] Extension poultry specialist. Although, he added, no bird species have been cloned yet.

In other animals in which cloning has been successful, the promise of creating herds of disease-resistant animals is appealing.

Creating such herds is a little more complicated than basic cloning—DNA first would need to be tinkered with to add immunity or delete susceptibility. But doing that successfully with an entire herd would be difficult, disease—might be a potential lure to the consumer market. But Whitelaw, one of the Roslin researchers, is skeptical about this, too.

Current practices of disease management, such as bringing only young cows to slaughter, greatly reduce the likelihood of mad cow disease. And this method is much cheaper than tinkering with an animal's genome in the laboratory.

First, the retired UW researcher, also pointed out that even if you could create herds resistant to all common ailments that afflict a particular breed, there's no way to keep them immune to everything.

If a new or rare disease were to strike a cloned herd, it could wipe it out.

Special Uses of Cloning

Woolliams, the Roslin geneticist, is betting that cloning will have its biggest impact as a means of preservation.

If the technology could be developed more cheaply and efficiently—current cloning procedures are wildly inefficient with hundreds of attempts made for every one successful clone—he believes it could enable farmers in developing nations to conserve breeds facing extinction.

Dotted around the world, small populations of rare breeds—such as the New Zealand Hokonui sheep or the British Red Poll cow—may harbor important genes for disease resistance or retain desirable characteristics that could be incorporated into improved breeds of livestock.

Woolliams said it's vital these breeds are preserved so there remains a genetic reservoir in which to tap.

If that's to happen, help likely will have to come from governments, conservation groups or other concerned organizations, because there probably isn't money to be made.

In the end, the researchers agree that cloning's use will be applicable only for special animals: pets, endangered species and a few, truly spectacular farm animals.

Cloning May Help to Save Endangered Species

Sylvia Pagán Westphal

Sylvia Pagán Westphal is a science journalist with a background in biology. In the following selection she describes the efforts that have been made to clone endangered animal species. This is a difficult process because with present animal cloning technology there are only a few live births from hundreds of implanted embryos; thus, many females must be used, which is not possible if a species is rare. It is therefore necessary to use related species as egg donors and surrogate mothers. Therefore, because a cloned animal carries some genes from the egg donor, it is not an exact replica of the original. Westphal states that no one yet knows whether this small number of foreign genes will alter an endangered species. She also writes that problems arise in deciding which endangered species to clone—the most popular animals, for which research funding can be obtained, are not necessarily the ones with which cloning would work best. So cloning alone cannot solve the problem preserving endangered species; Westphal maintains that other methods of saving them must be continued.

It is 2050 and only 30 cheetahs are left in the world. Tireless efforts to help the animals reproduce in the wild have failed and the species could soon die out. But there is a lifeline, and it's in the freezer. Scientists turn to thousands of cell samples collected from cheetahs over the years since 2002, and one by one each of these animals is reincarnated with the help of cloning. Welcome to the future of conservation.

This vision is anything but fantastical. If all else fails—such as habitat preservation or breeding programmes—clon-

Sylvia Pagán Westphal, "Copy and Save," *New Scientist,* June 19, 2004. Copyright © 2004 by Reed Elsevier Business Publishing, Ltd. Reproduced by permission.

ing could be rolled out as a last resort to save a species on the brink of extinction. The first endangered animal to be cloned was an ox-like beast called a gaur, native to India and parts of Asia, which was born in 2001. A handful of others have followed. Scientists are even getting close to cloning a species that is already extinct.

But although various projects have already adopted cloning as a tool for saving species, it is still surrounded by doubts and controversy. Fundamental questions about the technique and its effect on the resulting animals remain unanswered. Some of the projects centering on high-profile endangered mammals such as the giant panda are struggling to make progress, while creatures that could reap more benefits from cloning, such as fish or amphibians, are being ignored. Critics worry that cloning could be a distraction from the vital work of protecting habitats so that endangered species can recover naturally in the wild.

Despite the debate, the question is no longer whether cloning endangered species can ever work—it most likely will for species related to those that have already been successfully cloned, such as cows, goats, sheep, rabbits, cats and horses. The issue is whether it should be done, and if so, for what purpose. "Really, what is the conservation utility?" says geneticist Oliver Ryder from the Zoological Society of San Diego. "The big answer is we don't know yet if cloning can help the conservation efforts."

As soon as [the birth of] Dolly the sheep, the first mammal to be cloned, was [announced] in 1997, conservationists realised they had a new means of reproducing animals. For those struggling to coax vanishing species to breed in captivity, cloning seemed like a godsend. In theory, you could make a new individual by taking the genetic material of an endangered animal and placing it inside an egg whose own nucleus had been removed. This could then be stimulated to form an embryo, which you could in turn implant into a surrogate mother. A genetic replica of the original animal would then be born.

Cloning Endangered Species Is Difficult

But if regular cloning was inefficient and difficult, scientists knew that using the technique with endangered species would be even harder. Given cloning's dismal success rate (only a few live births from hundreds of implanted embryos), scientists would have to experiment on tens, possibly hundreds, of females. The rarity of endangered species means this is simply not an option. The only possibility would be to find a female from a related but more common species to serve as egg donor and surrogate mother. That would add an extra layer of difficulty to the whole process. Could it ever work?

The answer came with the birth of Noah, the cloned gaur, who had been created using a cow as both egg donor and surrogate. Although he died of a common infection two days after birth, Noah exemplified the power of cloning for conservation. Soon after came announcements of projects to clone the giant panda, the African bongo antelope, the Sumatran tiger (now abandoned) and the cheetah, among others.

For some of these species though, the obstacles seem insurmountable. Take the quest to clone the giant panda, of which approximately 1000 individuals are left in the wild. The project has been running for six years and has suffered major technical disappointments. In 2002, for example, the Chinese team in charge of the project published results of a series of attempts to implant cloned panda embryos. They used rabbits as a surrogate species, since panda cubs are only a few inches long at birth, about the same size as rabbit kits.

The team introduced DNA from panda cells into rabbit eggs and implanted some 2300 embryos into rabbit females. None resulted in pregnancy. The team then tried using cats as surrogates, and in a rather peculiar series of experiments each of 21 cats was implanted with 10 of the panda-rabbit cloned embryos and 10 cat-rabbit embryos (cat DNA in a rabbit egg). They yielded some early pregnancies, but none lasted past 48 days, compared with about 65 days for a normal cat gestation.

The leader of the Chinese team, Da-Yuan Chen, says the team has decided to shift gears and look for a better surrogate species—possibly a bear. But not everyone is as optimistic that this will be the solution. The China Wildlife Protection Association and other panda researchers in China now oppose the project and say that the technique of mixing cells and eggs from different species isn't advanced enough in the case of pandas.

Related Species Must Be Used as Donors and Surrogates

The only successful attempts to clone endangered animals have been those using closely related species as egg donors and surrogates. For example, in 2003 the Audubon Nature Institute of New Orleans in Louisiana announced the birth of three male clones of the African wildcat, and five females have just been born. The clones were created using domestic cats as egg donors and surrogate mothers. "in one year we will naturally breed them and show they can produce kittens," says researcher Betsy Dresser.

Similarly, the Zoological Society of San Diego in collaboration with Advanced Cell Technology of Massachusetts—the same company that created Noah—announced in 2003 the birth of two clones of a banteng, a wild forest ox from southeast Asia. The egg donor and surrogate species was the Angus cow. One of the clones has recently gone on display at the zoo, says Robert Lanza from Advanced Cell Technology.

But the truth is that nobody really knows how closely related two species need to be for this approach to work—rather a crucial question when various other high-profile cloning projects involve this kind of scenario. For example, scientists at the Laboratory for the Conservation of the Endangered Species in Hyderabad, India, are hoping to clone a cheetah, and are considering the leopard for the surrogate species.

However, some are more concerned with the end result of these efforts, should they succeed. Mixing genetic material from one species with an egg from another means the cloned animal will actually carry genes from both species. During the cloning step, the donor egg retains some of its power-generating mitochondria, and these contain their own DNA. A number of studies suggest that these mitochondria end up in the cloned organism, so an animal cloned in this way won't be an exact genetic replica of the original, even if these extra genes aren't actually in the nucleus.

"It is a big issue," says conservationist William Holt of the Zoological Society of London. "What you get out is not what you are trying to conserve." Dresser agrees in part, but adds that nobody knows whether this small number of genes will make a noticeable difference to the animal. "If the other choice is extinction I know what I am going to choose," she says.

Which Animals Should Be Cloned?

But even as scientists work to solve the technical challenges of cloning, one crucial question looms: how do you decide which animals to clone? More than 970 animal species, including 184 mammals, are believed to be at extremely high risk of extinction in the wild. Thousands more are threatened. Dresser says that one of the hardest things as a conservationist is accepting that logic is not always the deciding factor when making that choice. "It's all about funding. The public would rather fund a project with a tiger than a little brown frog," she says.

The trouble is that the most popular species could turn out to be the worst candidates for cloning. And some have dwindled to such low numbers that cloning might not be much help anyway, says Paul Bartels, head of the Wildlife Biological Resource Centre of the Endangered Wildlife Trust in Pretoria, South Africa. Once a species becomes too inbred, the animals become weaker and more prone to inherited genetic disease, though the issue of how low is too low is highly contentious. There have been cases in which successful breeding programmes have reintroduced a species to the wild after the population had gone down to only tens of individuals, argues Dresser.

Holt also believes that conservation's cloning efforts have overlooked the potential benefits for non-mammalian species—ironic considering that the very first cloning experiments, done in the 1950s and 60s, were performed on amphibians. Among vertebrates, mammals present the most challenges for cloning because it interferes with a genetic mechanism called imprinting, which only mammals rely on to develop properly. Mammals also require additional steps during embryo culture and implantation, as well as monitoring during pregnancy.

If the goal of conservation is to save as many species as possible with limited resources, wouldn't it make more sense to focus on amphibians or fish? After all, more of these species are disappearing, and assisted reproduction has been of little help. "it might be simpler to just go straight to cloning," says Holt. Scientists wouldn't face the imprinting issue or have to develop ways of implanting embryos, since fertilisation and development happen outside of the body, he adds.

Whatever the outcome of this debate, conservationists agree on one thing: cloning should not be seen as conservation's panacea. The technique is still in its early stages, so plans to clone an animal should only take place alongside other efforts to save a species. For example, Dresser says that during her team's work with the African wildcat, they also devised techniques for IVF [In Vitro Fertilization], embryo freezing and embryo transfer. "We have developed kittens with all of these," she says.

Cloning Could Help Maintain Genetic Diversity

But there is one area where cloning could play a key role once the technology has matured: maintaining the genetic diversity of rare species. Tissue from animals could be collected and frozen to be defrosted later and cloned to revitalise the gene pool. Hundreds of cell lines from threatened populations are already being stored in these "frozen zoos", a kind of insurance policy for the future. "If you have collected live cells from a population and suddenly they die out, you can bring back diversity," says Bartels.

South Africa's frozen zoo, BioBank SA, started collecting samples about two years ago and so far has a cache of cell lines from about 60 wild endangered species. And the Audubon Nature Institute's frozen zoo has collected cells from over 5000 individuals representing about 150 species, says Dresser. "Any time we get our hands on any animal at the zoo we take a skin biopsy and grow a cell line," she adds.

But the advantage of tissue banking reaches far beyond cloning. It can provide scientists with a way to monitor the genetic fitness of a declining population in order to decide when to take action, says Bartels. "You can go back to a sample from 10, 20, 30 years ago to redefine how your population is changing," he says. Banking also essentially buys time while scientists perfect cloning technology, and importantly, make it cheaper and more suitable for conservation. "It would be an incredible gift for the future," says Ryder.

Can Cloning Resurrect Extinct Species?

The billion-dollar question is, of course: can cloning help resurrect a species that has gone extinct? Japanese and Australian teams are aspiring to the ambitious goal of cloning extinct animals such as the woolly mammoth or the Tasmanian tiger, which died out in 1930. Most scientists agree these projects have little to do with conservation. The groups are not even close to achieving their goal, since they don't have cells to work with and so must first piece together fragmented DNA from remains.

However, José Folch and colleagues at the Agricultural Research Service in Zaragoza, Spain, have come close to recreating a bucardo, a type of mountain goat that became extinct in 2000 after the last member of the species was killed in an accident. The team is trying to clone the animal from cells taken while it was alive, using domestic goats as surrogates. Folch told *New Scientist* the team has achieved two pregnancies—one lasted 45 days and the other two months. Now the team is now fine-tuning the technology, though Folch says he can't forecast whether they will succeed.

Even if they do, it is unlikely they could ever resurrect the species. For one thing, scientists would have to create a male bucardo to mate with the cloned female. For another, the problems of inbreeding make re-establishing a viable population from just two individuals well nigh impossible. For these and other reasons, experts believe the projects like these can't be considered conservation. "They are entertainment," says Holt. Although cloning could help us conserve endangered species, it cannot salve humanity's conscience by raising the dead. Extinction is still forever.

Ethicists Debate the Cloning of Pets

Part I: R. Albert Mohler Jr.; Part II: Autumn Fiester

R. Albert Mohler Jr. is president of the Southern Baptist Theological Seminary in Louisville, Kentucky, and is a well-known columnist and radio/TV commentator. In Part I of the following selection he discusses the ethical problems raised by the first commercial cloning of a pet, a kitten named Little Nicky. Mohler believes not only that cloning pets is wrong, but that public acceptance of it might lead to acceptance of human cloning. In his opinion, cloning makes people forget that both humans and pets are more than the product of genetic determination. Autumn Fiester is the director of graduate studies in the Department of Medical Ethics at the University of Pennsylvania and a senior fellow at its Center for Bioethics. In Part II of this selection she argues that there is no need to worry about the welfare of cloned pets, as they will be loved and pampered. In her view, other potential forms of animal biotechnology are of far more serious concern.

Part I: R. Albert Mohler Jr.

Just before the end of [2004], headlines across the nation announced that a Texas woman had received delivery of a newly cloned kitten—an exact replica of the pet she had cherished for 17 years. The woman, identified only by her first name in press reports, declared herself ecstatic about the kitten and pleased to have paid the $50,000 required for the carbon copy of her beloved dead cat, "Nicky."

Part I: R. Albert Mohler Jr., "The Case of the Cloned Kitten—an Ethical Challenge," *Christian Post*, January 12, 2005. Originally published on www.albertmohler.com. Reproduced by permission. Part II: Autumn Fiester, "Cloning Beloved Pets Is the Least of Our Problems," www.bioethics.net, January 12, 2005. Copyright © 2005 by Autumn Fiester. Reproduced by permission.

The new kitten, dubbed "Little Nicky," was declared by a spokesman for Genetic Savings and Clone, Inc. to be "the world's first commercial pet clone."

Most readers saw the story as something of a curiosity. From a human interest angle, many must have wondered why any person would pay $50,000 just to clone a cat. A good many seemed to think that the woman should be free to do whatever she wants with her money, and some observers were even quick to defend the $50,000 cost of the cloned kitten as a legitimate response to the death of a beloved pet. Nevertheless, the cloned kitten pushes significant ethical issues onto the nation's agenda. Are we now to accept the cloning of pets as an acceptable use of scientific technology?

Genetic Savings and Clone

Of course, Little Nicky has a history. The company that produced the cloned kitten, Genetic Savings and Clone (GSC), based in Sausalito, California, was founded by John Sperling, an eccentric billionaire who attempted to influence the 2004 presidential campaign and years ago founded the University of Phoenix, the nation's most lucrative and successful for-profit university.

Sperling is no stranger to cloning technology. Several years ago, Sperling and his associates attempted to clone a dog. That unsuccessful attempt prompted him to fund research at Texas A&M University in 1998 that eventually produced a cloned kitten, known as "Carbon Copy" or "C.C." Over time, Sperling grew frustrated at the slow pace of progress at the university and established Genetic Savings and Clone in 2000. Little Nicky is the first product of a project the company is now undertaking. Last year, GSC launched its "Nine Lives Extravaganza," a cat cloning service intended to produce up to 50 cloned kittens over the next several months.

"For the first time in history, pet cloning is being offered to the public," the company's Web site declares. "Our gene banking clients have welcomed the announcement with great interest and enthusiasm." This last statement refers to the service the company offers which allows for genetic material to be "banked" for future use.

The company is not above sales hype, of course. "Our production capacity for 2004 is limited, so if you want to clone your cat this year, please contact us promptly for further details." The company promises "that the clones we produce for our clients will be consistently healthy and bear striking resemblance to their genetic donors." An official with the company indicated that a money-back guarantee would assure clients of satisfaction.

The "Nine Lives Extravaganza" package comes complete with a video documenting the cloning process, a "presentation party and dinner," and the opportunity to allow the company to publicize the event. Dog lovers should not feel left out, because the company "is actively engaged in the development of technology to clone dogs," expecting to offer the dog cloning services as early as [2005].

Little Nicky Is Troubling to Some

"Julie," as Little Nicky's owner has been identified, declared that her cloned kitten is virtually an exact replica of her dead pet. "He is identical. I have not been able to see one difference," she said. She later explained, "When Little Nicky yawned, I even saw two spots inside his mouth—just like Nicky had. Little Nicky loves water, like Nicky did, and he's already jumped into the bathtub like Nicky used to do." Yet, while Julie excitedly tells of Little Nicky's exploits in the bathtub, those more concerned with the ethical dimensions of this development are troubled by the use of cloning technology to reproduce pets.

David Magnus, co-director of the Center for Biomedical Ethics at Stanford University in California, told the press, "The whole premise of this operation is morally highly problematic. There is no good reason to do this when millions of pets have to be euthanized each year because they do not have homes and when this process carries unknown health risks to the animal." Furthermore, Magnus insisted that clients like Julie are "not getting what they think they're getting" when they pay to have their pets cloned. "These people are really having trouble accepting that death is a natural part of life and want an animal just like the one that died, but animals, just like humans, are more than just their genes."

Commenting on the prospect of cloned pets, Lawrence M. Hinman, director of the Values Institute and a professor of philosophy at the University of San Diego admitted that, since pet cloning is not dealing with human beings, "it has fewer of the moral issues associated with human cloning." Nevertheless, "pet cloning requires us to address the question of whether there is something morally objectionable about such cloning apart from the standard arguments about respect for life."

In the end, Hinman argued that the cloning of pets is ethically indefensible. "We can produce a genetically identical copy of our pet, but we delude ourselves if we think we have somehow accomplished something by this substitution. If I buy a clone of my dog, I get only a replica of the unique animal I loved. Isn't it more honest to move on, to build a new relationship with a new, unique animal rather than try to duplicate something from the past?"

Those We Love Are Not Replaceable

As Hinman went on to explain, "The loves of our lives are not interchangeable or replaceable, and the attempt to treat them as such will harm both them and us. We, and our pets, are more than the sum of our genes. To fail to understand this is to fail to understand ourselves and our relationships to those we love."

American ethicists were not the only authorities to raise ethical concerns. In Great Britain, the practice of cloning animals as pets is banned. Britain's Royal Society for the Prevention of Cruelty to Animals [RSPCA] has declared the practice "grossly immoral," pointing out that cloned animals stand a good chance of early death.

In Scotland, an official study released by the Church of Scotland responded to the cloning of "C.C." by denouncing the project. "The creation of a cloned cat at a university in Texas is an experiment which should not have been attempted—on animal welfare grounds and because it trivializes scientific research."

Making its point clearly, the church's statement went to the heart of the matter. "Just because a millionaire is prepared to fund such research, and potential pet owners are prepared to pay, does not justify doing it. It must also be justified ethically. Against this overall background, cloning pets seems ethically unacceptable. It is too trivial an intervention in one of our fellow creatures. This represents a waste of scientific skills and resources, which could be put to far better uses, like addressing human or animal disease." Furthermore, "Cloning is also a misplaced reaction to the loss of a beloved pet, because it would not re-create the same animal."

More Ethical Problems

These ethical concerns are well established in the scientific literature. An article in the scientific journal *Nature*, published shortly after the first successful cloning of a cat, acknowledged, "We can only roughly evaluate the efficiency of cloning cats by nuclear transfer," because "87 cloned embryos were transferred into eight recipients, resulting in one failed pregnancy and one live clone."

In other words, this first effort to produce a successfully cloned kitten required the creation of 87 cloned embryos which resulted in only two pregnancies—one that ended in failure.

The financial argument also has relevance, though it often betrays a rather contorted set of values. Some observers suggested that the $50,000 would have been better spent supporting animal shelters for abandoned pets. What about the very real needs of human beings?

The most significant ethical problem presented by the case of the cloned kitten is the use of clonal technology to reproduce a conscious being. In this case, the technology was used to create a cat. Next year, the company may be able to apply its commercial cloning service to dogs. What comes next?

Pet Cloning May Lead to Human Cloning

The most sinister aspect of this development is a likelihood that emotional, cultural, and ethical barriers to human cloning will be weakened by public acceptance of animal cloning. Once we become accustomed to cloning Fido and Felix, we can be assured that someone will soon argue that humans should have the right to clone relatives, friends, or heroes.

Furthermore, the entire project smacks of biological reductionism. We—and our pets—are more than our genes. This is true of animals, whose personalities are not merely the product of genetic determination. This is infinitely more significant in the case of human beings, made in the image of God, who are far more than genetically-determined organisms living out a genetically-determined script.

The cloning of Little Nicky, celebrated in the media and greeted with enthusiasm by some animal lovers, should trouble the nation's ethical conscience. At every level, this is an indefensible use of a dangerous technology. Regardless of this pet owner's emotional satisfaction in possessing a genetic replica of her dead pet, the greater danger is that this society will be left with unbridled technologies unhindered by this civilization's abandoned ethic.

Kittens today, dogs tomorrow . . . what comes next? Regrettably, we are likely to find out all too soon.

Part II: Autumn Fiester

Pet cloning is now officially a commercial enterprise. For the price of $50,000, a Texas woman commissioned a clone of her beloved cat "Nicky," and today she is the proud owner of that cat's genetic twin, aka "Little Nicky." The creation and sale of Little Nicky has sparked intense criticism from bioethicists across the country, who label the pet cloning venture everything from "frivolous" to "reprehensible." But in the unregulated land of animal biotechnology, cloning pets for devout animal lovers seems like the least of our animal welfare problems.

The most serious concern critics raise about pet cloning is the suffering of the clones, which are sometimes born with health problems or don't survive past infancy. But cloning science is advancing so rapidly that the survival rates and general health of clones are beginning to mirror animals naturally conceived. So this will soon be a non-starter.

What criticisms remain? The most common complaint is that it's wrong to spend $50,000 to clone a pet when millions of unwanted animals are euthanized in shelters each year. This is an odd argument for a lot of reasons. First, there's nothing different about this use of money and any other luxury purchase—the money could always be better spent if put towards noble causes like fighting world hunger or curing AIDS. This fact doesn't make pet cloning any different ethically than boat-buying. And why would a person who was devoted to a particular animal be more obligated than the rest of us to save others of that species—let alone members of other species? Finally, the criticism misses the point of pet cloning: pet owners don't want just any old cat. They see their original animal as a unique being, not one that's exchangeable. They spend the money on cloning because the closest they can come to getting that particular animal back is having the identical twin of their beloved pet.

Worry About Pet Clones Is Misplaced

If animal welfare worries are truly the motivation for critiquing cat cloning, then the concern is misplaced. Little Nicky, and other clones like him, will thrive and end up being some of the most pampered pets in America. What ought to really worry us is an animal biotechnology industry that is wholly unregulated and may have more imagination than good sense. The real "Frankenpets" are just around the corner: transgenic animals and chimeras that will be conglomerations of different species spliced together. The Glofish and Alba the Green Bunny are just the first in a long line. These animals will make run-of-the-mill cat cloning seem dull. But how much will these strange animals suffer? How will these animals impact other animals or the ecosystem? If we are going to put animal cloning on our moral agenda, it's not pet cloning that we should worry about.

Cloning Dogs May Lead to Cures for Human Diseases

Choe Sang-Hun

Choe Sang-Hun is a reporter in the Seoul, Korea, bureau of the Associated Press. The following selection is his news story about the announcement of the world's first cloned dog in August 2005. The dog, an Afghan hound named Snuppy, was cloned at Seoul National University. The aim was not to clone pets, but to develop technology for curing diseases in dogs that might eventually be used for curing human diseases. Although many animals, including cats, have been cloned in the past, dogs are harder to clone because female dogs' eggs are not as mature as those of other animals at the time of ovulation and must therefore be obtained from the oviducts rather than the ovaries. Other researchers had tried unsuccessfully to clone dogs, and so the South Korean scientists' achievement was a major breakthrough.

Snuppy, a 101-day-old Afghan hound, scampered on a rainsoaked lawn and nuzzled journalists' cameras at a university campus [in Seoul, South Korea, on August 3, 2005], presenting himself as proof that man could clone his best friend.

Snuppy, the world's first cloned dog, is another milestone for a team of South Korean stem cell experts who had stunned the world [in 2004 by announcing that they had cloned] a human embryo and gleaned stem cells from it, which theoretically could be directed to grow into any parts of a human body.[1]

On [August 3], the team led by Hwang Woo Suk and Lee Byeong Chun of Seoul National University announced that it had cloned the dog, considered one of the most difficult animals to clone. With human cloning ruled out as unethical, sci-

---

1. It was later learned that they had not really done this.

entists have been racing to master animal cloning, hoping that some day this would help them find cures for human diseases.

Hwang said the next step for his team was to develop dog stem cells and demonstrate that cloned stem cells in dogs were safe and effective for treating the naturally occurring diseases in dogs, like diabetes, cancer, sleeping disorder or dementia. These diseases are also found in humans.

"Wouldn't it be a marvelous thing that our best friend will be the first beneficiary of stem cell medicine? And in learning whether it's safe or effective in our companions, we may also know whether it is safe or effective for our loved ones," said Gerald Schatten, a professor of cell biology at the University of Pittsburgh School of Medicine. Schatten has consulted on Hwang's research.

South Koreans Support Stem Cell Research

The creation of Snuppy, short for Seoul National University puppy, is a testament to South Koreans' penchant for dedicating national resources to a sector they believe they can excel in globally. After semiconductors and shipbuilding, the latest focus is biotechnology.

While the public is divided over stem cell research in countries like the United States, [in South Korea it has] full govenerment backing....

Seoul also wants to turn South Korea into a global hub for stem cell research, endorsing Hwang's plan to open an international stem cell bank by October to help speed up the quest to grow replacement tissue to treat diseases.

Last week, the government approved a research project by a local genetic engineering lab that would harvest stem cells from frozen "leftover" human embryos in fertility clinics and attempt to grow them into specific cell types.

This was the first time Seoul had approved such a stem cell project since the country adopted a law in January that banned the cloning of human beings.

But the law allowed stem cell research for medical purposes. The health ministry has 27 research stem cell projects waiting for its review . . . .

To reach [the goal of curing human disease] Hwang said, stem cell research in animals was crucial.

"Sheep, cows, cats, goats, deer, mules, horses, rabbits, pigs and mice—all these animals have been cloned," Hwang said. "The dog had been the last domesticated animal that defied cloning, and we have surmounted the challenge."

Hwang posed with Snuppy and Tai, an Afghan hound from which Snuppy was cloned. Also present was Snuppy's surrogate mother, a yellow Labrador retriever.

South Koreans have an obsession with becoming the first in the world. The national pride in Hwang's work has prevented ethical battles.

The news release from the Ministry of Science and Technology had a nationalistic spin.

"This again proves that the animal cloning and biotechnology of South Korea is at the top of the world," the statement said.

Hwang, 52, grew up in a rural village and reportedly said that he had spent so much time with his family cow as a boy that he could communicate with it eye to eye. He asks for similar dedication to tasks from his 43-member team, known for working weekends and even sleeping in the laboratory.

Hwang Opposes Pet Cloning

Hwang's work is a breakthrough for the commercial pet-cloning industry in the United States. The first cloned-to-order pet sold in the United States was a 9-week-old kitten produced by the biotech firm Genetic Savings and Clone of Sausalito, California.

Hwang, who is applying for a patent on his team's technology, wants no part in the commercial pet-cloning industry.

He also called for a worldwide ban on human cloning, which he called "ethically outrageous" and "technically impossible."

"Cloned human beings are merely a science fiction fantasy," Hwang said last month.

Animal Cloning Paves the Way to Human Cloning

Gregory E. Pence

Gregory E. Pence is a professor in the philosophy department and School of Medicine at the University of Alabama. He is the author of several books and articles about genetic engineering and bioethics, and he has testified about cloning before congressional committees. In the following selection from his book Cloning After Dolly: Who's Still Afraid?, *he explains that cloning animals enables scientists to develop knowledge that is building a foundation for human cloning. Thus, Pence believes that the successful cloning of many animals shows that someday it may be safe to clone humans.*

For some, animal cloning is a sideshow to the main act of human cloning, a little warm-up act about rates of success and failure that may or may not generalize to cloning humans, the kind of thing that people in the agriculture business think about in terms of livestock, certainly not something relevant to humans. After all, experiments you can do on animals differ greatly from what you can do on humans. The two kinds of beings live in two different moral universes.

People who think this way are mistaken: animal cloning is paving the way to human cloning. Understanding the basics of mammalian genetics, physiology, and development is building the foundation for human cloning, just as countless animal studies have preceded human trials in medicine. Like it or not, humans are animals, and their genetics, physiology, and reproduction follow the patterns of other mammals. What we learn in general about mammalian cloning will directly translate to human cloning. Nevertheless, people think very differently about animal cloning and human cloning. Cloning animals such as pigs and rats is a curiosity, almost a freak show, not an important moral event; nothing like cloning a human child.

I think that view is naive. Biotechnology is pressuring the rigid lines between all kinds of species, adding a fish gene to a strawberry plant to prevent damage from frost and growing human embryos in cow eggs. Ignoring genetic incursions of human genes into nonhuman animals, as well as incursions going the other way, is to ignore one of the most important ethical topics of our day.

The first big picture is that the only good ethical objection to trying to originate a child by cloning is that it may produce a physically damaged child. But this objection is based on what we know at this early stage about animal cloning. As those facts change, the strength of the objection proportionally weakens. Eventually, if scientists can safely originate every other mammal by cloning, this will be good inductive evidence that human cloning is safe to try.

The second big picture concerns groups opposed to genetically modifying animals, either through cloning, knockout genes, or genetic enhancement. Humans have modified animals by breeding them for food and pets since prehistoric times, when friendly wolves became the ancestors of today's dogs and African wildcats became the ancestors of today's cats. We have been changing animals ever since for our food, for company, and to fulfill our desires. Whether that is moral is a big question, but biotechnology itself is only doing something in a more efficient way that has been done for centuries: selectively breeding animals for specific characteristics to fulfill human purposes. Before, creating a particular kind of fish, cat, cow, or dog was a hit-or-miss process, but now the process can be much more efficient.

Animal Successes

In 1995 scientists thought it was an exceptionless, unbreakable law of nature that animal cloning was impossible, but breakthroughs since the cloning of Dolly the sheep have been spectacular. Although the media harps on abnormalities and numbers of aborted fetuses, it never provides a context for these figures, for example, that one embryo has died for every human ever born, or that one in twenty humans is a twinless twin (one twin dying in utero).

In an amazingly short time after the announcement of Dolly's birth, researchers cloned several different animal species. In January 1998, just ten months later, Steve Stice of Advanced Cell Technology (ACT) announced that he and University of Massachusetts scientist James Robl had cloned two calves, Charlie and George, plus six identical twins, that grew up near Texas A&M in College Station. Stice and Robl founded ACT as a for-profit company and the identical calves were cloned to produce human serum albumin, a blood protein given to patients in hospitals. After Dolly, PPL Therapeutics created the lambs Molly and Polly to create factor IX, a blood protein that promotes blood clotting.

In June 1998, Ryuzo Yanagimachi, a biologist at the University of Hawaii, announced that he and his Team Yana had cloned three generations of mice. Yanagimachi had previously contributed to in vitro fertilization and in 2003 was one of fifteen people elected to the National Academy of Sciences. In July 2000, the Roslin Institute announced in *Nature*, while a rival team of Japanese scientists announced in *Science*, that it had cloned pigs. Roslin cloned the "five little piggies" that (it hoped) would go to market for xenografts, and Akira Onishi of Japan's National Institute of Animal Industry cloned Xena from another pig fetus. . . .

Scientists in Taiwan in 2002 cloned two identical descendants of an alpine goat that was a champion milk producer. Japan had already imported a herd of alpine goats that adapted well to its hotter climate. A year after their birth, visitors met the healthy twins at an international biotechnology convention hosted by Taiwan.

In 2003 French scientists successfully cloned a rat. Cloning a rat was a boon to scientific research because rats are used extensively in research, for example, testing drugs for hypertension and diabetes. Cloned rats will also serve as identical sources for experiments in knock-out genes, where a gene is deliberately deleted to study what happens in the adult animal. . . .

Cloning Champion Dairy Cows

Scientists first produced a cloned Holstein cow on June 11, 1999, at the University of Connecticut at Storrs. The cow, named Amy, had a genotype taken from the ear of a prize cow named Aspen. This asexual technique was used later by Japanese scientists to clone a prized bull. It bypasses the cumbersome, normal process of inducing superovulation, harvesting eggs, and introducing sperm.

Another extraordinary cow, Zita, produced ninety-five gallons a day of high-quality milk at two years of age. In 1997 Zita was ranked the number 1 Holstein in America. Zita became the ancestor of many cloned dairy cows. Demand for Zita's genetic material was so great that in 1997, when Zita's owner visited Japan, the dairy industry there saw cloning as the best way to revive its ailing cattle industry. The Japanese bought five of Zita's sons for $125,000.

As Zita aged, her owner worried about whether her cells would be potent in producing more embryos, and when he met a representative of ACT, which had created a new unit called Cyagra to clone valued livestock, he agreed to use Zita's cells to produce the first cloned calves. In early 2000, Cyagra used cells from Zita's ear to create twenty embryos. Winnowed to the best ten, these embryos were inserted into ten surrogate cows, where they gestated for thirty-five days, creating eight pregnancies. After 120 days, six died shortly before birth. Two healthy fetuses made it to birth, Cyagra Z and Genesis Z, on February 6, 2000. Two weeks before, Japanese scientists had announced the first grand-clone of a cloned bull, giving them three generations of the same genotype.

A year later, Cyagra cloned a descendant from a prized Wisconsin cow named Mandy and then auctioned it off for $82,000. . . .

Cloned Racing Mules and Horses

The world took notice in May 2003 when a five-year project at the University of Idaho had a mare give birth to a normal mule created from a cloned embryo. Idaho Gem was the first member of the equestrian family to be cloned. Mules traditionally result from breeding a male donkey to a female horse. "A mule can't do it himself, so we thought we would give it a hand," said Gordon L. Woods, the lead scientist. Idaho Gem's birth occurred about the time that Americans embraced the horse Funny Cide, the gelding that won the Kentucky Derby and the Preakness but failed to win the Belmont and thus missed the Triple Crown. With equestrian cloning now possible, Funny Cide might have descendants. . . .

Three months after Idaho Gem's birth, Italian researcher Cesare Galli achieved the birth of the world's first cloned horse. Galli called the foal "Prometea" after the Greek god Prometheus. "Like Prometheus who took fire from God from Olympus, we hoped she would be brave to face these people who do not like what we do," he told reporters. Galli may have a way to go before conventions change. The Jockey Club, which controls horse racing in America, now forbids the racing of any horse that was cloned, as does the American Quarter Horse Association.

Prometea came from a single skin cell of her ancestor. In a first, her genetic ancestor was also her gestating mother. Some skeptics had claimed that a female could not bear her own twin because some minor genetic difference was needed for successful gestation. This skepticism was proven to be super-stition, not fact, as Prometea grew successfully for the full eleven months and arrived in perfect health. As usual, Galli had started with a higher number of pregnancies (four from seventeen implanted embryos), two of which spontaneously aborted and one of which miscarried halfway through.

Cloning is best thought of as a tool in the life sciences that, once perfected, can be used in many ways; in itself it is neither good nor bad. Although cloned horses currently are not allowed to race, horse cloning is a tool that allows for some new possibilities: geldings could be reproduced and their descendants could produce sperm. And although geld-ings can't reproduce and cloned horses can't race, what about a cloned horse from a gelding put out to stud? Would the sexually created descendants also be banned from racing or would they be allowed to race? The Jockey Club will soon need to answer such questions.

Horse cloning could also aid varieties of wild horses that are endangered, helping nature by reintroducing strong wild horses. Finally, many horse competitions do not ban cloned horses, such as jumping, dressage, harness and barrel racing. Perhaps the greatest demand for cloned horses might come from ordinary people who want a piece of greatness. If Seabis-cuit were still alive, wouldn't demand be high for his cloned twin-descendants?

Of course, the nature versus nurture debate will rear its head here, and this might be an easy place to start real stud-ies. People will swear right away that no clone of Seabiscuit will ever run as fast as Seabiscuit because of Seabiscuit's unique upbringing, experiences, and bonds with his jockey. Ditto for Secretariat, Alydar, and Seattle Slew.

But we shall see. People have a lot of emotion invested in their views. Since breeders know that clones of these horses have the genetic potential to be great, they might take extraordinary care to create exactly the right conditions for maximal potential. And they might get lucky very early or we might figure out the science very early, and regularly produce horses whose times match or beat their ancestors. If not, it will be an early test of how important the environment is to ultimate physical performance. And that too will teach us something important.

Did Dolly the Sheep Age Prematurely?

Critics of cloning such as MIT's Rudolph Jaenisch claim that because of reprogramming errors in the creation of the cloned embryo, no cloned mammals are normal, including Dolly and the champion cows described above. Such claims about Dolly have a political context and pedigree, which is worth understanding, so we digress for a moment to discuss the claim that Dolly was "six years old at birth" as well as the claim that "she died early because of cloning."

In addition to false claims that Dolly had not really been cloned from a differentiated cell, there was speculation, beginning when Dolly was three years old, that cloning caused her to age prematurely. A study released by the Roslin Institute in June 1999 showed that Dolly's telomeres were 20 percent shorter than normal lambs at the same age.

Telomeres are located at the ends of chromosomes and are speculated to be indicators of cell aging. They protect chromosomes from injury when cells divide. In most cells, the telomeres get shorter each time that cell divides. In humans, telomeres divide about twenty times over a lifetime, and in cows, sixty times. The number of times cells divide in a species is called the Hayflick limit. Telomeres are like a shell around an egg, and when the shell has eroded, this chromosomal egg breaks. This breakage may start many diseases of old age.

News circulated widely in 1999 that Dolly had shorter telomeres. "Three-year-old Dolly has 9-year-old body!" headlines screamed. But fewer headlines ensued when other researchers found that the telomeres of cloned calves were longer than normal, suggesting not premature aging but a fountain of youth. In August 2000, Dr. Robert Lanza, chief scientist at the famous for-profit firm, Advanced Cell Technologies (ACT) in Worchester, Massachusetts, announced that he had studied the telomeres of his cloned calves and found not shorter but longer telomeres. The team of famed Hawaiian researcher Ryuzo Yanagimachi also found the same good effects over five generations of cloned mice.

Although Lanza's and Yanagimachi's results excited some attention in the press, they were generally lost in the mass of many announcements about cloned animals and stem cells. Unfortunately most people still have the false impression that Dolly was old at birth. A similarly politicized story made the rounds at Dolly's death. Lambs living free in pastures may live twelve or thirteen years, so when Dolly had to be euthanized at age six, critics predictably sharpened their knives and had a feast. . . .

Dolly's Early Death Was Not Due to Cloning

Dolly's early death was most likely iatrogenic—caused by those around her, not a pathology in the way she was originated. . . . Always sought out by tourists and journalists, Dolly learned to stand on her hind legs and beg for food, which she usually got. So she grew fat and, as any pet owner knows, a heavy dog or cat putting weight on its back legs can experience injury late in life. . . .

After six years of hysteria over cloning in the mass media, veteran journalists learned to discount the sky-is-falling talk about cloning—in this case, hyperventilations about Dolly's premature death from cloning. . . .

Science writer Gina Kolata of the *New York Times* writes,

For Dolly, life was good. Her first 10 months, she shared a stall with two other sheep, but she would grab their food and she soon began growing fat. She would assert her authority by turning over her trough as soon as she finished eating and placing her forefeet on it, puffing out her chest and preening. Deciding that Dolly was not good at sharing, the Roslin staff finally put her in a stall by herself. While most sheep are shy around humans and huddle at the back of their pens when visitors arrive, Dolly loved attention. She rushed to the front of her stall when she saw people coming by, bleating loudly.

Dolly most likely died at an early age because she contracted a virus from being raised indoors. Her arthritis probably came from being overweight and standing too long in positions that are bad for sheep.

Are Cloned Animals Abnormal?

What about most cloned livestock? If Dolly and other cloned sheep are normal, what about cloned cows and bulls? Are most cloned cows and bulls abnormal? Jaenisch claimed that all cloned mammals are abnormal. If that is true, there is something odd about what has been going on in the livestock industry. One would think that companies paying $82,000 for a clone of Zita or Mandy would know by now that the dairy cow they bought was a freak and an abnormal producer of milk. But that is not the case. At least with cows, bulls, and lambs, reprogramming errors are not occurring. . . .

Fifty years of stories about zombie clones, slave clones, mindless soldier clones, spare organ clones, and other stories assuming cloned humans are abnormal or subhuman have combined with the evidence of the first years of cloning that born human babies likely will have some congenital defects. These two fronts, weird clones from science fiction and initial abnormal babies from the first mammals cloned, together convince virtually everyone, even scientists such as Wilmut and Jaenisch, that human reproductive cloning is inherently wrong.

Mark Westhusin, a researcher at Texas A&M University, cloned eighteen identical Brahmin bulls when he worked at Granada, including the famous rodeo bull Chance, and the famous cat CC ("Carbon Copy") at Texas A&M. Westhusin thinks that Jaenisch's claim that cloned animals are abnormal due to errors of epigenetic reprogramming is false. Westhusin's views are shared by animal researchers Steve Stice at the University of Georgia, who cloned the calves Charlie and George, and Jose Cibelli of Michigan State, who briefly grew a human nucleus in a cow egg while employed at ACT. . . .

As already noted, cloned animals are not a sideshow to the main event. In many ways, they are the main event, and for good reason. If there is truly "no such thing as a normal clone," then we are a long way from safely cloning humans. On the other hand, if expectations and ideology influence how people see cloned animals, then time may tell a different story.

Therapeutic Cloning of Human Embryos for Medical Research

Cloned Embryos Are Human Beings

Robert P. George and Alfonso Gómez-Lobo

Robert P. George is a professor of law and director of the James Madison Program in American Ideals and Institutions at Princeton University. Alfonso Gómez-Lobo is a professor of philosophy at Georgetown University. The following selection is a personal statement appended to the 2002 report on cloning issued by the President's Council on Bioethics, of which they are members. This statement presents arguments for the belief that cloned human embryos, even at a very early stage, are complete human beings and should therefore be given full moral respect—meaning that they should not be used as a mere means to benefit others. In the opinion of Professors George and Gómez-Lobo, the destruction of human embryos for medical research is wrong and should be banned.

Fertilization produces a new and complete, though immature, human organism. The same is true of successful cloning. Cloned embryos therefore ought to be treated as having the same moral status as other human embryos.

A human embryo is a whole living member of the species homo sapiens in the earliest stage of his or her natural development. Unless denied a suitable environment, an embryonic human being will by directing its own integral organic functioning develop himself or herself to the next more mature developmental stage, i.e., the fetal stage. The embryonic, fetal, infant, child, and adolescent stages are stages in the development of a determinate and enduring entity—a human being—who comes into existence as a single cell organism and develops, if all goes well, into adulthood many years later. . . .

Robert P. George and Alfonso Gómez-Lobo, "Statement of Professor George," *Human Cloning and Human Dignity,* by the President's Council on Bioethics. Washington, DC: President's Council on Bioethics, 2002.

Embryos Are Complete Organisms

The adult human being that is now you or me is the same human being who, at an earlier stage of his or her life, was an adolescent, and before that a child, an infant, a fetus, and an embryo. Even in the embryonic stage, you and I were undeniably whole, living members of the species homo sapiens. We were then, as we are now, distinct and complete (though in the beginning we were, of course, immature) human organisms; we were not mere parts of other organisms.

Consider the case of ordinary sexual reproduction. Plainly, the gametes whose union brings into existence the embryo are not whole or distinct organisms. They are functionally (and not merely genetically) identifiable as *parts* of the male or female (potential) parents. Each has only half the genetic material needed to guide the development of an immature human being toward full maturity. They are destined either to combine with an oocyte or spermatozoon to generate a new and distinct organism, or simply die. Even when fertilization occurs, they do not survive; rather, their genetic material enters into the composition of a new organism.

But none of this is true of the human embryo, from the zygote and blastula stages onward. The combining of the chromosomes of the spermatozoon and of the oocyte generates what every authority in human embryology identifies as a new and distinct organism. Whether produced by fertilization or by SCNT [somatic cell nuclear transfer] or some other cloning technique, the human embryo possesses all of the genetic material needed to inform and organize its growth. Unless deprived of a suitable environment or prevented by accident or disease, the embryo is actively developing itself to full maturity. The direction of its growth *is not extrinsically determined* but is in accord with the genetic information *within it*. The human embryo is, then, a whole (though immature) and distinct human organism—a human being.

If the embryo were *not* a complete organism, then what could it be? Unlike the spermatozoa and the oocytes, it is not a part of the mother or of the father. Nor is it a disordered growth such as a hydatidiform mole or teratoma. (Such entities lack the internal resources to actively develop themselves to the next more mature stage of the life of a human being.) Perhaps someone will say that the early embryo is an intermediate form, something that regularly emerges into a whole (though immature) human organism but is not one yet. But what could cause the emergence of the whole human organism, and cause it with regularity? It is clear that from the zygote stage forward, the major development of this organism is *controlled and directed from within*, that is, by the organism itself. . . .

Do Embryos Deserve Full Moral Respect?

But does this mean that the human embryo is a human being deserving of full moral respect such that it may not legitimately be used as a mere means to benefit others?

To deny that embryonic human beings deserve full respect, one must suppose that not every whole living human being is deserving of full respect. To do that, one must hold that those human beings who deserve full respect deserve it not in virtue of *the kind of entity they are*, but, rather, in virtue of some acquired characteristic that some human beings (or human beings at some stages) have and others do not, and which some human beings have in greater degree than others.

We submit that this position is untenable. It is clear that one need not be *actually* conscious, reasoning, deliberating, making choices, etc., in order to be a human being who deserves full moral respect, for it is clear that people who are asleep or in reversible comas deserve such respect. So, if one denied that human beings are intrinsically valuable in virtue of what they are, but required an additional attribute, the additional attribute would have to be a capacity of some sort, and, obviously a capacity for certain mental functions. Of course, human beings in the embryonic, fetal, and early infant stages lack immediately exercisable capacities for mental functions characteristically carried out (though intermittently) by most (not all—consider cases of severely retarded children and adults and comatose persons) human beings at later stages of maturity. Still, they possess in radical (= root) form these very capacities. Precisely by virtue of *the kind of entity they are*, they are from the beginning actively developing themselves to the stages at which these capacities will (if all goes well) be immediately exercisable. In this critical respect, they are quite unlike cats and dogs—even adult members of those species. As humans, they are members of a natural kind—the human species—whose embryonic, fetal, and infant members, if not prevented by some extrinsic cause, develop in due course and by intrinsic self-direction the immediately exercisable capacity for characteristically human mental functions. Each new human being comes into existence possessing the internal resources to develop immediately exercisable characteristically human mental capacities—and only the adverse effects on them *of other causes* will prevent their full development. . . .

We can, therefore, distinguish two senses of the "capacity" (or what is sometimes referred to as the "potentiality") for mental functions: an immediately exercisable one, and a basic natural capacity, which develops over time. On what basis can one require for the recognition of full moral respect the first sort of capacity, which is an attribute that human beings acquire (if at all) only in the course of development (and may lose before dying), and that some will have in greater degree than others, and not the second, which is possessed by human beings as such? We can think of no good reason or nonarbitrary justification.

Natural Capacity for Mental Functions

By contrast, there are good reasons to hold that the second type of capacity is the ground for full moral respect.

First, someone entertaining the view that one deserves full moral respect only if one has immediately exercisable capacities for mental functions should realize that the developing human being does not reach a level of maturity at which he or she performs a type of mental act that other animals do not perform—even animals such as dogs and cats—until at least several months after birth. A six-week-old baby lacks the *immediately exercisable* capacity to perform characteristically human mental functions. So, if full moral respect were due only to those who possess immediately exercisable capacities for characteristically human mental functions, it would follow that six-week-old infants do not deserve full moral respect. If one further takes the position that beings (including human beings) deserving less than full moral respect may legitimately be dismembered for the sake of research to benefit those who are thought to deserve full moral respect, then one is logically committed to the view that, subject to parental approval, the body parts of human infants, as well as those of human embryos and fetuses, should be fair game for scientific experimentation.

Second, the difference between these two types of capacity is merely a difference between stages along a continuum. The proximate, or immediately exercisable, capacity for mental functions is only the development of an underlying potentiality that the human being possesses simply by virtue of the kind of entity it is. The capacities for reasoning, deliberating, and making choices are gradually developed, or brought toward maturation, through gestation, childhood, adolescence, and so on. But the difference between a being that deserves full moral respect and a being that does not (and can therefore legitimately be dismembered as a means of benefiting others) cannot consist only in the fact that, while both have some feature, one has more of it than the other. . . .

All Humans Are Equally Valuable

Third, being a whole human organism (whether immature or

not) is an either/or matter—a thing either is or is not a whole human being. But the acquired qualities that could be proposed as criteria for personhood come in varying and continuous degrees: there is an infinite number of degrees of the relevant developed abilities or dispositions, such as for self-consciousness, intelligence, or rationality. So, if human beings were worthy of full moral respect only because of such qualities, and not in virtue of the kind of being they are, then, since such qualities come in varying degrees, no account could be given of why basic rights are not possessed by human beings in varying degrees. The proposition that all human beings are created equal would be relegated to the status of a superstition. . . . Clearly, developed self-consciousness, or desires, or so on, are arbitrarily selected degrees of development of capacities that all human beings possess in (at least) radical form from the coming into being of the organism until his or her death. So, it cannot be the case that *some* human beings *and not others* are intrinsically valuable, by virtue of a certain degree of development. Rather, human beings are intrinsically valuable *in virtue of what (i.e., the kind of being) they are*; and *all* human beings—not just some, and certainly not just those who have advanced sufficiently along the developmental path as to be able to exercise their capacities for characteristically human mental functions—are intrinsically valuable.

Since human beings are intrinsically valuable and deserving of full moral respect in virtue of what they are, it follows that they are intrinsically valuable from the point at which they come into being. Even in the embryonic stage of our lives, each of us was a human being and, as such, worthy of concern and protection. Embryonic human beings, whether brought into existence by union of gametes, SCNT, or other cloning technologies, should be accorded the status of inviolability recognized for human beings in other developmental stages. . . .

Research Cloning Is Morally Worse than Reproductive Cloning

In conclusion, we submit that law and public policy should proceed on the basis of full moral respect for human beings irrespective of age, size, stage of development, or condition of dependency. Justice requires no less. In the context of the debate over cloning, it requires, in our opinion, a ban on the production of embryos, whether by SCNT or other processes, for research that harms them or results in their destruction. Embryonic human beings, no less than human beings at other developmental stages, should be treated as subjects of moral respect and human rights, not as objects that may be damaged or destroyed for the benefit of others. We also hold that cloning-to-produce-children ought to be legally prohibited. In our view, such cloning, even if it could be done without the risk of defects or deformities, treats the child-to-be as a product of manufacture, and is therefore inconsistent with a due respect for the dignity of human beings. Still, it is our considered judgment that cloning-for-biomedical-research, inasmuch as it involves the deliberate destruction of embryos, is morally worse than cloning-to-produce-children. Thus we urge that any ban on cloning-to-produce-children be a prohibition on the practice of cloning itself, and not on the implantation of embryos. Public policy should protect embryonic human beings and certainly not mandate or encourage their destruction. An effective ban on cloning-to-produce-children would be a ban on all cloning.

Cloned Embryos Are No More than Cells

Ronald Bailey

Ronald Bailey is a science correspondent for Reason *magazine.
His articles have appeared in many magazines and he is the author of several books, most recently* Liberation Biology: The Scientific and Moral Case for the Biotech Revolution. *In the following selection he argues that the human embryos from which
stem cells are derived are not persons. In Bailey's opinion, early
embryos could be considered persons only if every cell in the human body were considered a potential person, since every cell
contains a complete set of DNA and through cloning technology
could be developed into a baby.*

Congress is considering legislation that would criminalize
stem cell research, punishing researchers with 10 year jail
terms and $1 million fines. [This legislation did not pass.] The
health of millions is in the balance.

Proponents of the research, including 80 Nobel Laureates,
argue that stem cells derived from human embryos could possibly cure a host of degenerative illnesses such as Parkinson's
disease, arthritis, diabetes, heart disease, and cirrhosis of the
liver. "It is not unrealistic to say that [stem cell research] has
the potential to revolutionize medicine," says former National
Institutes of Health Director Harold Varmus in *Newsweek*.

Opponents, while acknowledging the cures, respond that
using stem cells is immoral because, in their view, the cells
can only be derived by killing the tiniest and most helpless of
human beings. As Ken Connor, president of the Family Research Council, has said, "We believe very strongly that people

Ronald Bailey, "Are Stem Cells Babies?" *Reason Online,* July 11, 2001. Copyright ©
2001 by the Reason Foundation, 3415 Sepulveda Blvd., Suite 400, Los Angeles, CA
90034, www.reason.com. Reproduced by permission.

should not be discriminated against based on age or location in the petri dish."

Currently, human embryonic stem cells are derived from donated frozen embryos left over from in vitro [outside the body] fertilization procedures. That may be changing, and sooner than we think.... A study published in *Fertility and Sterility* [in 2001] revealed that a fertility clinic in Norfolk, Virginia, has created embryos using donor eggs and sperm specifically for the purpose of deriving stem cells. The researchers argue that specifically creating embryos to derive stem cells is, in their view, less ethically problematic because such embryos are never intended to be implanted in a woman's womb and so were never intended to become babies.

Embryos, whether donated or specifically created, are grown in petri dishes for about a week, at which point they have divided into a microscopic, hollow ball of about 100 cells. Researchers then remove the inner cell mass, the cells of which can differentiate into all the kinds of tissues in a human body.

Stem cells can be transformed into any kind of tissue and used to repair organs damaged by strokes, trauma, and degenerative diseases. Researchers at Geron Corporation claim to have learned how to turn human embryonic stem cells into 110 different kinds of cells, including heart muscle, neurons, and immune system cells.

Each Cell in the Body Could Become a Person

So what about the claims that incipient therapies based on human embryonic stem cell research are immoral? That brings us to the question of whether the embryos from which stem cells are derived are persons. The answer: Only if *every* cell in your body is also a person.

Why? Because scientific ingenuity now makes it logically (if not quite logistically) possible for each of your body's cells to become your twin.

Each skin cell, each neuron, each liver cell is *potentially* a person. All that's lacking is the will and the application of the appropriate technology. Cloning technology like that which famously produced the Scottish sheep Dolly in 1997 could be applied to each of your cells to potentially produce babies (a mammary cell was used to create Dolly).

Cloning technology at this point in time is clunky. In the future, though, researchers will likely be able to skip cloning, and simply flip few genetic switches to regress any of your cells to earlier stages of development, claims Harold Varmus, former director of the National Institutes of Health. After all, each of your cells contains the complete genetic code which produces you. Ultimately, researchers could take your cells all the way back to the embryonic stage, at which point they could be implanted into a womb, where they could eventually develop into complete human beings.

Why go on about the fate of your skin and liver cells that are destined to be sloughed off during your next shower or die of alcohol poisoning at your next cocktail party? Clearly, they are not going to become your twins. Ah, but they *could*, if only you would let them.

"What happens when a skin cell turns into a totipotent stem cell [a cell capable of developing into a complete organism] is that a few of its genetic switches are turned on and others turned off," writes University of Melbourne bioethicist Julian Savulescu in the April 1999 issue of the *Journal of Medical Ethics*. "To say it doesn't have the potential to be a human being until its nucleus is placed in the egg cytoplasm [i.e., cloning] is like saying my car does not have the potential to get me from Melbourne to Sydney unless the key is turned in the ignition."

Developing a Baby Requires a Suitable Environment

Like turning the key in the ignition to begin a journey, simply starting a human egg on a particular path, either through fertilization or cloning, is a necessary condition for developing a human being, but it isn't sufficient. A range of other conditions must also be present. Those conditions include the availability of a suitable environment such as a woman's womb. (Some 40 percent of embryos produced naturally do not implant and so never develop into babies.)

Two well known pro-life politicians understand that "certain conditions" make a difference. According to *Newsweek*, Sen. Orrin Hatch (R-Utah) argues that "a frozen embryo stored in a refrigerator in a clinic" isn't the same as "a fetus developing in a mother's womb." Connie Mack, former Republican senator from Florida, declares, "For me, as long as that fertilized egg is not destined to be placed in a uterus, it cannot become life." In other words, for Hatch and Mack, location in a petri dish makes a lot of difference.

"I cannot see any intrinsic morally significant difference between a mature skin cell, the totipotent stem cell derived from it, and a fertilised egg," writes Savulescu. "They are all cells which could give rise to a person if certain conditions obtained."

"If all our cells could be persons, then we cannot appeal to the fact that an embryo could be a person to justify the special treatment we give it," concludes Savulescu.

The DNA content of a skin cell, a stem cell, and a fertilized egg are exactly the same. The difference between what they are and what they could become is the environment in which their DNA is found. Thus, the mere existence of human DNA in a cell cannot be the source of a relevant moral difference. The differences among these cells are a result of how the genes in each are expressed, and that expression depends largely on which proteins suppress or promote which genes.

So people who oppose stem cell research must logically be committed to the notion that the only difference between your skin cell and your twin are the proteins that decorate their DNA strands. But can moral relevance really be reduced to the presence or absence of certain proteins in a cell?

Stem Cells from Cloned Embryos Could Help Cure Disease

John C. Avise

John C. Avise is a professor of genetics at the University of Georgia. In the following selection, he explains the concept of therapeutic cloning (sometimes called research cloning or somatic cell nuclear transfer (SCNT)). In this process, the nucleus would be removed from a human egg and replaced with the DNA from a patient in order to obtain embryonic stem cells genetically matched to that patient, which could be used for organ or tissue transplants. Although it is the same process used to clone animals, the egg would not grow into a fetus; it would be used only to produce a mass of cells grown in vitro (outside the body). However, some people consider it unethical to use human embryonic cells for medical purposes, and it is therefore controversial. In some countries research is proceeding, while in others it has been banned. In the United States such research is legal, but federal funds cannot be used for it.

More than 40 years have elapsed since Joseph Murray and his colleagues at a Boston hospital successfully transplanted a kidney between identical twins. This landmark approach was later extended by the medical community to other organs (e.g., heart, liver, lung, and pancreas) and to transplants involving more distant relatives and unrelated individuals. Transplants between unrelated individuals are especially challenging because, unless ameliorative actions are taken, the immune system of a transplant recipient sooner or later re-

John C. Avise, *The Hope, Hype, and Reality of Genetic Engineering: Remarkable Stories from Agriculture, Industry, Medicine, and the Environment.* New York: Oxford University Press, 2004. Copyright © 2004 by Oxford University Press, Inc. Reproduced by permission.

jects the alien cells. To alleviate this problem, donor and recipient typically are matched as closely as possible for genes underlying immune responses, and immunosuppressive drugs also are administered. Such procedures are fairly common and have saved many lives. Nonetheless, modern transplantation surgery remains risky due to inherent immunological intolerances of patients to foreign tissue.

Thus, many research professionals are excited about "therapeutic cloning," a new GM [genetic modification] approach that in theory should avoid the immunorejection problem. In this procedure, genes in cells to be transplanted originate from the patient, who therefore serves in effect as both donor and recipient. Because the donor and recipient tissues have identical genotypes, presumably the immune system would not recognize the implanted tissue as alien. Another reason for enthusiasm about therapeutic cloning is that this approach gives scientists welcome opportunities for basic research on human genetic disorders as they unfold during cell and tissue development.

How Therapeutic Cloning Works

The notion of therapeutic cloning for tissue or organ reconstruction in humans traces to the development of nuclear-transfer [NT] cloning methods for sheep and other farm animals. As applied to human cells, the procedure might work as follows: A suitable cell is removed from a patient and its nucleus is inserted physically into an enucleated egg. The egg then begins to multiply in a test tube, and, from the developing mass, pluripotent cells (those that possess a capacity to differentiate into multiple tissue types) are induced to grow replacement cells needed by the patient. Nerve cells might be grown to treat Alzheimer's disease or spinal cord injuries, skin cells could be used to repair burn damage, retinal cells for macular degeneration, pancreatic cells for diabetes, hematopoietic cells for leukemia, neuroglia cells for multiple sclerosis, and so on. When returned to the patient's body, the cloned cells in such tissues or organs ideally would repair or replace the damaged body part, without evoking immunological rejections.

Several technical challenges must be overcome before this approach is medically viable. First, NT techniques developed for farm animals will have to be improved and adapted to our species. Second, cells in the proliferating mass must be generated in such a way that they indeed are pluripotent at the outset. Third, the developmental potential of those flexible cells then must be channeled to produce the specialized kind of tissue that the patient requires. Fourth, methods must be devised to put those now-dedicated cells together properly to make a therapeutically useful tissue or organ. This may take place naturally when the cells are placed in a patient's body, or in some cases it may be accomplished initially *in vitro* [outside the body]. For example, replacement skin tissue for burn victims might be constructed by seeding the cloned cells onto sheets of a polymeric scaffolding substance. Finally, tissue therapy must be conducted such that the cloned cells do no harm when returned to the patient. It would be disastrous, for example, if even a few cells in the transplanted tissue began to divide in an unregulated, cancerous fashion.

Ethical Issues

Of course, ethical issues will have to be addressed as well. When the initial oocyte created by NT begins to divide into two cells, then four, then eight, and so on, when does the cloned mass become a new human being worthy of protection under the law? Opponents of therapeutic cloning often contend that an individual arises at the exact moment that the first cell appears, such that any sacrifice of an early cell mass, even for medical purposes, is tantamount to slaughter. Proponents of therapeutic cloning view this notion as nonsense. How, they ask, can a few amorphous cells be granted legal rights that take precedence over those of sentient human beings in desperate need of cell therapy? Remarkably, in U.S. society, most of the debate over the possible legalization of therapeutic cloning hinges on this one emotion-laden philosophical issue.

In such public discussions, a common error (or often, an intentional argumentative ploy) is to equate therapeutic cloning with reproductive cloning. Although the initial laboratory steps in the two procedures are identical—both begin by inserting a cell nucleus into an unfertilized egg—that is where the similarity ends. In reproductive cloning, the GM egg would be reimplanted in the womb and allowed to grow into a fetus and baby, the intent being to generate a fully functional and independent human being genetically identical to its predecessor. In therapeutic cloning, the early clump of preimplantation cells that comes from the GM egg would be grown *in vitro* and used to produce replacement tissues for medical rehabilitation.

After open deliberations, if a democratic society decides to ban therapeutic cloning on moral grounds, so be it. However, it would be a great shame if that decision arose merely from semantic confusion between therapeutic and reproductive cloning. For this reason, and because the word cloning itself carries such emotional baggage, some people have suggested that "therapeutic cloning" be replaced by less provocative phrases such as nuclear transplantation, tissue rejuvenation, or NT cell therapy. Indeed, if the word cloning had never been used by researchers in the context of NT cell therapy, quite likely this medical procedure would not have catapulted so forcefully into the public and political spotlight.

The artificial cloning of cells for therapeutic purposes offers some of the greatest possibilities in all of genetic medicine for saving human lives and improving the health of countless citizens. Thus, I find it horribly sad, as well as ironic, that this promising new approach has been met with strident social and political opposition in the United States. Tragically, opponents of therapeutic cloning, who would elevate the rights of cells above those of sentient human beings, might possibly cause our nation to squander this marvelous opportunity for improving human health.

Embryonic Stem Cells

During normal sexual reproduction, the nucleus of a fertilized egg or zygote contains two nearly matched sets of genetic material, one from each of the two parents. This never-before-seen mixture of genes will interact to direct an individual's biological development, from pre-embryo to the person's death perhaps decades later. However, in the first two to four rounds of cell division, most of the RNA and protein molecules that orchestrate initial development are critical holdovers that were produced and deposited into the egg cytoplasm (the envelope surrounding the nucleus) by the mother's genome. Much of the primary activation in the zygotic genome occurs after a ball of about 4–16 pre-embryonic cells has formed.

After further cell-division rounds (each roughly doubling the total number of cells), a fluid-filled cavity begins to form within the growing cell-ball. This hollow sphere, known as a blastula or blastocyst, consists initially of about 100 cells. To one side of its central cavity is a knob of undifferentiated cells, the "inner cell mass," from which embryonic stem (ES) cells are derived. They eventually will give rise to all of the 260 or so cell types that make up a person's tissues, organs, and body structures.

The entire blastocyst, still floating free in the mother's reproductive tract, finally implants into the female's uterus during the second week after fertilization. Then the differentiation of the embryo's body parts begins in earnest. For example, a heart takes shape and begins beating by week four. One week later, the embryo reaches a length of about one-third of an inch. By week eight, rudimentary precursors to all body structures in the adult are present, and the developing individual is termed a fetus. By the end of the first trimester (12 weeks), the two-inch long fetus becomes recognizably human (as opposed to another animal). By the end of the second trimester (24 weeks), the fetus is almost a foot long, and at about 40 weeks a baby is born.

The initial happenings are basically the same under therapeutic cloning via nuclear transfer, except that in therapeutic cloning the nuclear genome of the zygote is a replica of the nuclear genome of the donor somatic cell, rather than a novel amalgamation of genes from an egg and a sperm. Under therapeutic cloning, however, development of the early cell mass occurs *in vitro* and is truncated at the preimplantation stage, when ES cells are harvested and grown for medical purposes. It is the pluripotency of ES cells, their ability to differentiate into multiple cell and tissue types, that makes these cells valuable as wellsprings for tissue rejuvenation. In principle, ES cells for research or medical purposes can also be obtained from naturally produced pre-embryos or embryos. Indeed, such surplus specimens are discarded routinely at fertility clinics conducting *in vitro* fertilizations. Regardless of how ES cells are obtained, once isolated they can be grown in laboratory cell culture more or less indefinitely. However, stem cell lines do tend to become less functional and less viable over time.

How Stem Cells Could Be Used

When exposed to particular environmental stimuli *in vivo* [inside the body] or *in vitro*, ES cells spontaneously differentiate into any of a variety of cell types, such as muscle, pancreas, skin, or liver. Scientists have identified several ways to manipulate ES cells grown in culture so that they develop into particular lineage types. For example, applying retinoic acid tends to channel ES cells to become neurons; serum albumin and other factors can stimulate ES cells to differentiate into blood cells; and "protein 4" induces ES cells to form mesenchymal cells that when naturally present in the living body produce connective tissues or transport vessels of the circulatory and lymphatic systems. However, far more research will be necessary before we learn how such ES cells might be harnessed to medically relevant tasks.

About 4 million Americans have Alzheimer's disease, 1.5 million have Parkinson's, and 200,000 suffer with serious spinal cord injuries. These are just a few of the individuals and medical conditions that might be early candidates for therapeutic treatments using ES cells to regenerate damaged tissues. But in the United States, opposition to stem cell research has been stiff in some circles. President George W. Bush, for example, has stated that he is opposed to cloning of any sort, and Leon Kass, whom Bush appointed to chair a National Bioethics Commission (to advise the president on biomedical issues and be "the conscience of our country") is also a gut-level opponent. Recently, that commission produced a mixed vote on whether therapeutic cloning should be banned. An advisory panel of the National Academy of Sciences, the most august scientific organization in America, issued a 2001 report affirming support for therapeutic cloning (while also calling for a ban on reproductive cloning). Polls suggest that the U.S. public is also strongly in favor of ES cell research for medical purposes.

A Political Decision

In a decision with huge sociopolitical as well as scientific ramifications, President Bush then decreed that federal funds not be used for research on ES cells other than those from an estimated 64 cell lines that purportedly were available in August 2001 (the usable number actually turned out to be far lower, perhaps ten or fewer). Many researchers in the United States view this ban as a serious impediment to medical advances because of insufficient genetic variety as well as limited availability of government-approved stem cell lines. The construction of additional cell lines has since been taken up without federal support, for example, at Stanford University.

Some observers hailed the 2001 Bush decision as a reasonable compromise between two competing ethical concerns (i.e., that harvesting ES cells is equivalent to embryonic murder, and that a complete ban on ES research would deny millions of disabled children and adults the therapeutic potential of tissue rejuvenation). Others interpreted the Bush decision as political pander to religious conservatives, an action that will seriously impede health care in the United States and drive key medical research overseas. Saudi Arabia, China, England, and Malaysia are among the countries actively considering therapeutic cloning of ES cells as a part of their own medical biotechnology initiatives.

I have already stated where I stand on these issues. My hope is that ethically responsible research into therapeutic cloning, if otherwise left unfettered, will help lead human medicine into a much brighter future.

The Chance of Medical Benefits from Cloning Is Remote

Mark Derr

*Mark Derr is a writer who has published articles in many maga-
zines and is the author of several books. He has Parkinson's disease, for which many people believe a cure might be found
through therapeutic cloning. Derr does not agree with that view.
In this selection, he explains why he opposes human cloning research. He is troubled by the fact that scientists are justifying it
by predictions of potential benefits that he considers overly optimistic. He does not think it offers much hope for a cure, and
states that even if it did, he would rather give it up than rush
into a practice to which, in his opinion, there are moral, ethical,
economic, and scientific objections.*

After I was diagnosed with Parkinson's disease two years
ago, at the relatively young age of 52, I read everything I
could about the condition's usual "progression"—an odd word
for degeneration. The worst-case prognosis is grim: a long
slide into physical and mental incapacity.

That is not going to happen to me, I said, as I began measuring my physical decline. I am young enough that I may be
able to benefit from advances in medicine, especially in brain
research. Maybe with new medications I would be able to put
off taking L-dopa, the best drug for Parkinson's but one that
loses its effectiveness over time. Surely better treatments will
become available, I told myself.

So why didn't I welcome the news that researchers in South
Korea were able to clone a human embryo and extract viable
stem cells from it? After all, one of the researchers said their
goal was "not to clone humans, but to understand the causes

of diseases"—and one of the diseases named most often was Parkinson's. Scientists say they may one day find a way to develop stem cells into brain cells to replace the ones that are killed or disabled by Parkinson's.

Part of my reaction, I know, is simply personal; I don't think cloning offers much hope for a cure for Parkinson's any time soon. But my objections are also moral, ethical, economic and scientific.

Potential Benefits Are Overstated

I feel this way not because I oppose human cloning, although I do. What bothers me is that scientists are putting forth an overly optimistic list of potential benefits of their research. The potential benefits of human cloning, we are told, include growing replacement kidneys and other organs, nerve cells to patch damaged spinal cords, and neurons to help cure neurodegenerative diseases like Parkinson's.

Such predictions engender genuine, if speculative, hope. I suspect it is human nature to want to believe in a cure, whether derived through magic or science. But ethical uneasiness clouds this promise when the issue is human cloning.

If the researchers crossed an heretofore unbreachable line by cloning a human embryo, the argument goes, they did so for a noble cause. Neither they nor any other respectable scientist would engage in reproductive cloning to create a human baby. By implication, if I object to therapeutic human cloning I am condemning myself—and everyone else with an incurable disease—to a life of suffering. I am also opposing scientific progress.

But the invocation of human suffering to justify cloning and other controversial procedures is disingenuous and unfair. Saying that their goal is therapeutic does not alter the fact that researchers in South Korea have cloned an embryo that could become a human being. [After this article was written, it was found that those researchers' claim to have cloned embryos was untrue.] Holding out the possibility of some future health benefit simply obscures more fundamental issues.

And the possibility of a health benefit seems remote. Even if researchers could use embryonic cloning to create neurons from my cells, who is to say that the new neurons won't die again after being injected into my brain? In trials so far, the injection of neurons from other sources into the brains of Parkinson's patients has largely failed to have an effect, perhaps because no one yet fully understands how the brain malfunctions in people with Parkinson's disease.

Medical Benefits Might Not Be Affordable

Even if cloning and implanting neurons worked, it would be expensive, with little guarantee that insurance companies would pay for it. Would the medical benefits of cloning be available only to those who could afford to pay for them? Someone like me might have to serve as a scientific guinea pig, a role I would prefer not to play.

Granted, stem cells from cloned embryos might provide scientists with some basic insights into the development of organs and cells, and might ultimately present the opportunity for testing treatments. But in its current state embryonic cloning means less to me, as a Parkinson's patient, than other new research, some of which involves adult stem cells. In a recent issue of the journal *Nature*, for example, researchers discussed the need to better understand the purpose and potential of neural stem cells that are found in all adult human brains.

For me, the tradeoff is personal. I would rather give up any possible benefit of human cloning research than rush into a practice with such profound repercussions for society. So why not declare a worldwide moratorium at least on human cloning? Scientists could study the cloned animals and embryos that now exist to determine their properties and potential. And the rest of us could join in the necessary debate about what it means to be human.

Therapeutic Cloning Is Urgently Needed

Gregg Wasson

Gregg Wasson is a former lawyer who is disabled by Parkinson's disease. The following selection is his testimony before the Senate Committee on the Judiciary as a patient advocate on behalf of the Coalition for the Advancement of Medical Research (CAMR). In it, he explains that his disease is presently incurable, that 100 million Americans are affected by disabling diseases, and that many of them hope that therapeutic cloning may lead to a cure. In his opinion, ignoring the potential of this research would be a tragic mistake. He also points out that therapeutic cloning is very different from reproductive cloning, and that he believes fears that it will lead to black-market reproductive cloning are unwarranted.

The potential of regenerative medicine is something that's important to my life. My name is Greg Wasson and I am here on behalf of the Coalition for the Advancement of Medical Research (CAMR). CAMR is comprised of universities, scientific and academic societies, patient's organizations, and other entities that are devoted to supporting stem cell research.

My task today is to attempt to represent the voice of millions of Americans living with MS [multiple sclerosis] ALS [amyotrophic lateral sclerosis] Parkinson's Disease, and many other illnesses who believe in the promise of regenerative medicine, including therapeutic cloning.

I, along with the Coalition for the Advancement of Medical Research (CAMR), support every effort to criminalize and ban human reproductive cloning. It's unsafe and unethical.

Gregg Wasson, testimony before the U.S. Senate Committee on the Judiciary, Washington, DC, March 19, 2003.

However, it is imperative that we protect therapeutic cloning. As a person living with Parkinson's disease, I know how urgently a cure is needed. Responsibly regulated regenerative medical research may one day provide better treatments and cures for a number of debilitating and presently incurable conditions.

Eight years ago, at age 43, I was diagnosed with Parkinson's disease. My fiancée, Ann Campbell, who is here with me today, was given the same diagnosis that same year at age 38. I was a lawyer in San Francisco. Ann was an editor and children's book author in New York City. Within five years we were both forced by our disease to retire on disability. Recently, I was also diagnosed with diabetes, a disease that runs in my family.

Advocacy for a cure of our shared disease brought us together. Clearly our vision is for science to bring about a life that is not plagued by this terrible disease so we can enjoy the rest of our lives together in health. Like millions of other Americans we need your help to make sure that our hope is not forsaken.

Parkinson's Disease Is Presently Incurable

An estimated 1 million Americans have Parkinson's, a brain disorder that is presently incurable and the cause of which is unknown. Parkinson's is a progressive and degenerative disease that slowly robs its victims of dopamine, the neurotransmitter that enables us to initiate and regulate movement. Walking, breathing, speaking, swallowing, simply grasping an object, all depend on a sufficient supply of dopamine to transmit the impulses of the brain into action.

Cognitive functioning, thinking, is also impaired by Parkinson's. It is often cognitive impairment that forces people with Parkinson's to stop working. This was the case for both Ann and myself. We also live with the knowledge that 30% of all Parkinson's patients develop dementia, and that we are three times as likely as the general population to develop Alzheimer's.

After eight years, we have difficulty controlling symptoms such as tremor, stiffness, rigidity, gait, and balance, even though we take several different Parkinson's medications. Currently, I take about 25 pills per day just for Parkinson's, and must redose every 3 hours.

My medications, which cost about $11,000 per year including diabetes medications, allow me to sit here before you today, and speak, and be understood. I am thankful for these medications. Without them, I would be unable to walk, feed or clothe myself. But my 25 Parkinson's pills every day do nothing to slow the progress of my disease. What you see when you look at me today is a medical marvel, but also an illusion—a "chemical costume" I must put on every 3 hours to create the impression of even imperfect health.

Parkinson's medications become less effective over time, which causes different problems for each patient. In my case, I now fluctuate "off" my medications without warning several times each day. An "off" fluctuation can leave me stranded at a mall, or in my living room, or at the movies. . . .

And for both Ann and myself, the time will come when our medications fail us permanently and we will be totally functionally disabled. At that time we will leave the world that we all currently inhabit, and enter a twilight world of immobility, encased in our bodies as if in tombs, able to think but not speak, understand but not communicate. Eventually some complication of the disease will cause death, a death that may by then be welcome.

Disabling Diseases Affect 100 Million Americans

And we are not alone. Parkinson's is just one of a score of chronic diseases and conditions that are fatal at worst and leave their victims permanently disabled at best. These diseases and conditions affect more than 100 million Americans. Each of us here today has a loved one or friend who has a disease such as Alzheimer's, ALS, MS, Diabetes or Parkinson's. These are terrible illnesses with dire consequences for their victims.

In 2001 I worked on a stem cell petition with a number of persons suffering from ALS, who became my friends. Now, two years later, most of them are dead. John Davis, an Alabama ALS victim and fellow advocate, once said of embryonic stem cell research, "this dog will hunt." He meant that such research had the potential to save countless lives, and he was right. But this research "will hunt" only if it is not leashed and muzzled. I believe that the same applies to SCNT [somatic cell nuclear transfer, the process used in cloning].

We are not without hope. Regenerative medicine, including responsibly regulated therapeutic cloning, may lead to a cure or treatment for Parkinson's disease and a host of other diseases and conditions. . . . Human reproductive cloning and cloning for therapeutic medical purposes are not the same scientifically, or otherwise. They have entirely different objectives. The creation of stem cells through SCNT . . . is a process that occurs entirely in a petri dish. Cell division is caused by electrical or chemical stimulation rather than the natural joining of sperm and egg. The resulting ball, perhaps 100 cells the size of a pinhead, is neither a human life nor anything near it. The use of SCNT does not destroy human life—it is an attempt to restore human life.

Ann Campbell and I, along with millions of other Americans, are people—living human beings—with terrible diseases that will kill us unless cures are found. The willingness of some here to sacrifice these lives, placing less value on them than on a chemically produced, unfertilized mass of cells perhaps grown from one of our own hair follicles is the real crime, the real shame.

Ignoring the Potential of Therapeutic Cloning Would Be a Mistake

Compassion and common sense must prevail; ignoring the potential of therapeutic cloning would be a national tragedy and a huge mistake. But as with other scientific advances in history, a vocal and well-organized minority is trying to stop this research. Galileo, Columbus, and a high school teacher named John Scopes [who was put on trial for teaching evolution], all held scientific beliefs that frightened their contemporaries. But the earth does revolve around the sun, the earth is round, and the theory of evolution is now widely accepted as scientific fact. Today the target is therapeutic cloning.

Opponents of stem cell research that employs therapeutic cloning have insisted that there are no studies showing its potential to treat disease. But numerous experts in the field, including witnesses who testified earlier today, have shown that this is not true.

Opponents have also argued that expressly legalizing therapeutic cloning will open the floodgates to a black-market in reproductive cloning. The history of organ transplantation demonstrates that this concern is unwarranted. When organ transplantation was new, objections were raised that it would lead to black markets in harvested organs. This did not occur, and today organ transplantation is strictly and effectively regulated.

Senators, we believe that you understand and appreciate the enormity of the potential for saving human beings from fates such as Parkinson's, ALS, diabetes, and spinal cord injuries. We believe that, individually and collectively, you will make the choice to protect and to restore life. What greater legacy could any government leave its citizens?

And so, because we have hope and faith that this country will recognize the value of research into regenerative medicine, Ann and I are getting married this fall. On our wedding day, we will raise a glass to the promise of a new day when diseases like Parkinson's are simply a terrible memory.

In this committee, in the Senate, and in Congress, we place our highest hopes and trust.

Therapeutic Cloning Would Lead to Human Reproductive Cloning

Stuart Newman

Stuart Newman is a professor at New York Medical College and a board member of the Council for Responsible Genetics. In the following selection, he argues that acceptance of medical research using cloned embryonic stem cells would lead to the use of cloned embryos that are more than clumps of cells in the future. In his opinion, cells derived from embryos eight or nine weeks old instead would offer even greater medical benefits, and someday, after people are used to the idea of using them, they might even approve of using tissue from viable fetuses for medical purposes. Although few today would go along with this possibility, let alone some of the more extreme ones that are suggested by experiments with animals, Newman thinks future generations might feel differently if they grew up in a world in which cloned embryos were routinely used for spare parts.

Advocates of research using cloned human embryos claim that the path to curing many of humankind's most terrible afflictions will be found through the production of embryonic stem cells that are genetically matched to prospective patients. But what is not generally appreciated is how, by simply following the logic of scientific and medical reasoning, the way would be paved for a "Brave New World" in which cloning technology will eventually be extended to produce even fully-developed clonal humans.

More than two decades of work on mouse embryo stem cells has yielded just a handful of published studies showing modest therapeutic results—in all cases less than what has

Stuart Newman, "Cloning's Slippery Slope," *GeneWatch*, September 2002. Copyright © 2002 by the Council for Responsible Genetics. Reproduced by permission.

been achieved with grafts of non-embryonic cells, including "adult" stem cells. Despite great efforts, embryo stem cells rarely become just one cell type or coherent tissue, but differentiate instead into disorganized mixtures of cell types. Most importantly, they are genetically unstable; when placed in adult mice, they produce tumors. Similar technical obstacles and risks would pertain to the use of embryo stem cells in human patients. These problems may be overcome by additional research. But this would undoubtedly take many years, and technologies, like water, tend to follow the path of least resistance.

Cells from Older Embryos Would Offer Benefits

Embryo stem cells are derived from embryos that are less than two weeks old—often described by advocates of experimental cloning as "a clump of cells in the bottom of a Petri dish." But scientists at Johns Hopkins University have isolated a different kind of human stem cell. These "embryo germ cells" are derived from embryos eight to nine weeks old and, like embryo stem cells, can differentiate into all cell types. Most importantly, when transplanted into experimental animals they do not cause cancer.

On purely scientific grounds, embryo germ cells show greater promise than embryo stem cells. If they were derived from clonal embryos they would be ideal candidates for the proposed regenerative therapies—and if the supporters of experimental cloning were candid, they would also be advocating research into sustaining clonal embryos for eight to nine weeks so that genetically matched embryo germ cells could be harvested. Such embryos could, of course, no longer be characterized as clumps of cells in a Petri dish.

Some supporters of the use of later embryos may reason that it is better not to raise all these possibilities from the start: once we have clonal embryos for a while and have become used to the idea, who would turn a deaf ear to calls by patients for even better therapeutics? And once stem cell harvesting from two-month clonal embryos was in place, who could resist the pleas to extend the time-frame so that liver and bone marrow could be obtained from six-month clonal fetuses to cure victims of life-threatening blood disorders such as beta-thalassemia, or so that brain lining cells could be harvested from near-term fetuses to treat people with Parkinson's disease? Earlier this year a Massachussets company reported a "proof of principle" in which tissues from clonal cow fetuses were shown to be tolerated as grafts by their adult genetic prototypes.

Where Would the Line Be Drawn?

All of this makes perfectly good scientific and medical sense. The only thing that stands in its way are standards of social acceptability concerning the uses to which developing human embryos and fetuses may be put. These, of course, may be quite different from views on the acceptability of ending a pregnancy when a woman decides to do so. Regarding utility, some may draw the line at the clump of cells; others at the two-month embryo; still others somewhat short of full-term.

A prominent British biologist has advocated producing headless human clones for spare body parts. Few engaged in the current debate would go along with the more extreme possibilities—but what about future generations, growing up in a world in which clonal embryos are routinely produced for spare parts? An example of the medical incentives to bring full-born clones to term can be discerned from a mouse study ... conducted [in 2002] by researchers at MIT [Massachusetts Institute of Technology]. These investigators started with a strain of mice lacking a gene needed for functioning of the immune system and used nuclear transfer from these mice (i.e., cloning) to make embryos and then embryo stem cells. They corrected the gene deficiency in some of the stem cells and then employed a method which allowed them to produce complete embryos containing only the corrected cells. The resulting mice were genetically identical to the nuclear donor, but with a repaired gene. These germ line–modified clonal mice were then used as bone marrow donors for the original impaired mice.

Full-Term Cloning Would Become Acceptable

Large sectors of the public have already accepted the idea that a couple can have a child to provide tissues for another, sick child, and this has actually been done in several well-publicized cases. The MIT study shows that, in principle, you can make the second child by cloning the first, with genetic corrections. This provides a motivation for full-term cloning that would not be viewed as sinister; indeed, it would be welcomed by many—and the technology exists to bring it off. Once the cloning of human embryos is underway, the spread of the technology will make it all but impossible to stop short of any of these applications.

Many supporters of research and "therapeutic" cloning, particularly those in the Senate, the scientific societies, and patient advocacy groups, have condemned the prospect of full-term cloning and stated that it should be banned. In this they have the support of the majority of Americans and of all international groups that have considered this issue. But the examples above show just how short-lived any such half-measure is likely to be.

CONTEMPORARY
ISSUES
COMPANION

CHAPTER 4

The Prospect of Human Reproductive Cloning

Human Cloning Would Be Damaging to Society

President's Council on Bioethics

The President's Council on Bioethics was created by President George W. Bush to advise him on ethical issues related to advances in biomedical science and technology. The chairman of the council, Leon R. Kass, is an M.D. and a professor at the University of Chicago as well as a Fellow in Social Thought at the American Enterprise Institute, a conservative policy research institute. He is well known for his many books and essays on biomedical ethics. The following selection comes from the Council's report Human Cloning and Human Dignity. *The council is strongly opposed to human reproductive cloning. In the opinion of its members, the cloning of children would diminish human dignity and would lead to impairment of those children's perception of individuality, as well as to troubled family relations. Furthermore, the council members believe that even if only a few children were cloned, there would be bad effects on society as a whole.*

Beyond the matter of procreation itself, we think it important to examine the possible psychological and emotional state of individuals produced by cloning, the well-being of their families, and the likely effects on society of permitting human cloning. These concerns would apply even if cloning-to-produce-children were conducted on a small scale; and they would apply in even the more innocent-seeming cloning scenarios, such as efforts to overcome infertility or to avoid the risk of genetic disease. Admittedly, these matters are necessarily speculative, for empirical evidence is lacking. Nevertheless, the importance of the various goods at stake justifies trying to think matters through in advance. . . .

President's Council on Bioethics, *Human Cloning and Human Dignity.* Washington, DC: President's Council on Bioethics, 2002.

Problems of Identity and Individuality

Cloning-to-produce-children could create serious problems of identity and individuality. This would be especially true if it were used to produce multiple "copies" of any single individual, as in one or another of the seemingly far-fetched futuristic scenarios in which cloning is often presented to the popular imagination. Yet questions of identity and individuality could arise even in small-scale cloning, even in the (supposedly) most innocent of cases, such as the production of a single cloned child within an intact family. Personal identity is, we would emphasize, a complex and subtle psychological phenomenon, shaped ultimately by the interaction of many diverse factors. But it does seem reasonably clear that cloning would at the very least present a unique and possibly disabling challenge to the formation of individual identity.

Cloned children may experience concerns about their distinctive identity not only because each will be genetically essentially identical to another human being, but also because they may resemble in appearance younger versions of the person who is their "father" or "mother." Of course, our genetic makeup does not by itself determine our identities. But our genetic uniqueness is an important source of our sense of who we are and how we regard ourselves. It is an emblem of independence and individuality. It endows us with a sense of life as a never-before-enacted possibility. Knowing and feeling that nobody has previously possessed our particular gift of natural characteristics, we go forward as genetically unique individuals into relatively indeterminate futures.

Living Up to Expectations Would Be a Burden

These new and unique genetic identities are rooted in the natural procreative process. A cloned child, by contrast, is at risk of living out a life overshadowed in important ways by the life of the "original"—general appearance being only the most obvious. Indeed, one of the reasons some people are interested in cloning is that the technique promises to produce in each case a particular individual whose traits and characteristics are already known. And however much or little one's genotype *actually* shapes one's natural capacities, it could mean a great deal to an individual's *experience* of life and the expectations that those who cloned him or her might have. The cloned child may be constantly compared to "the original," and may consciously or unconsciously hold himself or herself up to the genetic twin that came before. If the two individuals turned out to lead similar lives, the cloned person's achievements may be seen as derivative. If, as is perhaps more likely, the cloned person departed from the life of his or her progenitor, this very fact could be a source of constant scrutiny, especially in circumstances in which parents produced their cloned child to become something in particular. Living up to parental hopes and expectations is frequently a burden for children; it could be a far greater burden for a cloned individual. The shadow of the cloned child's "original" might be hard for the child to escape, as would parental attitudes that sought in the child's very existence to replicate, imitate, or replace the "original."

It may reasonably be argued that genetic individuality is not an indispensable human good, since identical twins share a common genotype and seem not to be harmed by it. But this argument misses the context and environment into which even a single human clone would be born. Identical twins have as progenitors two biological parents and are born together, before either one has developed and shown what his or her potential—natural or otherwise—may be. Each is largely free of the burden of measuring up to or even knowing in advance the genetic traits of the other, because both begin life together and neither is yet known to the world. But a clone is a genetic near-copy of a person who is already living or has already lived. This might constrain the clone's sense of self in ways that differ in kind from the experience of identical twins. . . . The crucial matter, again, is not simply the truth regarding the extent to which genetic identity actually shapes us—though it surely does shape us to some extent. What matters is the cloned individual's *perception* of the significance of the "precedent life" and the way that perception cramps and limits a sense of self and independence.

Concerns Regarding Manufacture

The likely impact of cloning on identity suggests an additional moral and social concern: the transformation of human procreation into human manufacture, of begetting into making. By using the terms "making" and "manufacture" we are not claiming that cloned children would be artifacts made altogether "by hand" or produced in factories. Rather, we are suggesting that they would, like other human "products," be brought into being in accordance with some pre-selected genetic pattern or design, and therefore in some sense "made to order" by their producers or progenitors.

Unlike natural procreation—or even most forms of assisted reproduction—cloning-to-produce-children would set out to create a child with a very particular genotype: namely, that of the somatic cell donor. Cloned children would thus be the first human beings whose entire genetic makeup is selected in advance. True, selection from among existing genotypes is not yet design of new ones. But the principle that would be established by human cloning is both far-reaching and completely novel: parents, with the help of science and technology, may determine in advance the genetic endowment of their children. To this point, parents have the right and the power to decide *whether* to have a child. With cloning, parents acquire the power, and presumably the right, to decide *what kind* of a child to have. Cloning would thus extend the power of one generation over the next—and the power of parents over their offspring—in ways that open the door, unintentionally or not, to a future project of genetic manipulation and genetic control. . . .

Production of Children to Specifications

The problem with cloning-to-produce-children is not that artificial technique is used to assist reproduction. Neither is it that genes are being manipulated. We raise no objection to the use of the coming genetic technologies to treat individuals with genetic diseases, even in utero—though there would be issues regarding the protection of human subjects in research and the need to find boundaries between therapy and so-called enhancement. The problem has to do with the control of the entire genotype and the production of children to selected specifications.

Why does this matter? It matters because human dignity is at stake. In natural procreation, two individuals give life to a new human being whose endowments are not shaped deliberately by human will, whose being remains mysterious, and the openendedness of whose future is ratified and embraced. . . . The uncontrolled beginnings of human procreation endow each new generation and each new individual with the dignity and freedom enjoyed by all who came before. . . .

By contrast, cloning-to-produce-children—and the forms of human manufacture it might make more possible in the future—seems quite different. Here, the process begins with a very specific final product in mind and would be tailored to produce that product. Even were cloning to be used solely to remedy infertility, the decision to clone the (sterile) father would be a decision, willy-nilly, that the child-to-be should be the near-twin of his "father." Anyone who would clone merely to ensure a "biologically related child" would be dictating a very specific form of biological relation: genetic virtual identity. In every case of cloning-to-produce-children, scientists or parents would set out to produce specific individuals for particular reasons. The procreative process could come to be seen increasingly as a means of meeting specific ends, and the resulting children would be products of a designed manufacturing process, products over whom we might think it proper to exercise "quality control." ...

One possible result would be the industrialization and commercialization of human reproduction. Manufactured objects become commodities in the marketplace, and their manufacture comes to be guided by market principles and financial concerns. When the "products" are human beings, the "market" could become a profoundly dehumanizing force. Already there is commerce in egg donation for IVF [in vitro fertilization], with ads offering large sums of money for egg donors with high SAT scores and particular physical features.

The concerns expressed here do not depend on cloning becoming a widespread practice. The introduction of the terms and ideas of production into the realm of human procreation would be troubling regardless of the scale involved; and the adoption of a market mentality in these matters could blind us to the deep moral character of bringing forth new life. Even were cloning children to be rare, the moral harms to a society that accepted it could be serious.

Prospect of a New Eugenics

For some of us, cloning-to-produce-children also raises concerns about the prospect of eugenics or, more modestly, about genetic "enhancement." We recognize that the term "eugenics" generally refers to attempts to improve the genetic constitution of a particular political community or of the human race through general policies such as population control, forced sterilization, directed mating, or the like. It does not ordinarily refer to actions of particular individuals attempting to improve the genetic endowment of their own descendants. Yet, although cloning does not in itself point to public policies by which the state would become involved in directing the development of the human gene pool, this might happen in illib-

eral regimes, like China, where the government already regu-
lates procreation. And, in liberal societies, cloning-to-produce-
children could come to be used privately for individualized
eugenic or "enhancement" purposes: in attempts to alter (with
the aim of improving) the genetic constitution of one's own
descendants—and, indirectly, of future generations.

Some people, in fact, see enhancement as the major purpose of cloning-to-produce-children. . . .

Cloning Would Lead to Genetic Enhancement

"Private eugenics" does not carry with it the dark implications
of state despotism or political control of the gene pool that
characterized earlier eugenic proposals and the racist eugenic
practices of the twentieth century. Nonetheless, it could prove
dangerous to our humanity. Besides the dehumanizing pros-
pects of the turn toward manufacture that such programs of
enhancement would require, there is the further difficulty of
the lack of standards to guide the choices for "improvement."
. . .

The "positive" eugenics that could receive a great boost
from human cloning, especially were it to be coupled with
techniques of precise genetic modification, would not seek to
restore sick human beings to natural health. Instead, it would
seek to alter humanity, based upon subjective or arbitrary
ideas of excellence. The effort may be guided by apparently
good intentions: to improve the next generation and to enhance the quality of life of our descendants. But in the process
of altering human nature, we would be abandoning the standard by which to judge the goodness or the wisdom of the
particular aims. We would stand to lose the sense of what is
and is not human.

The fear of a new eugenics is not, as is sometimes alleged,
a concern born of some irrational fear of the future or the
unknown. Neither is it born of hostility to technology or nos-

talgia for some premodern pseudo-golden age of superior naturalness. It is rather born of the rational recognition that once we move beyond therapy into efforts at enhancement, we are in uncharted waters without a map, without a compass, and without a clear destination that can tell us whether we are making improvements or the reverse. The time-honored and time-tested goods of human life, which we know to be good, would be put in jeopardy for the alleged and unknowable goods of a post-human future.

Troubled Family Relations

Cloning-to-produce-children could also prove damaging to family relations, despite the best of intentions. We do not assume that cloned children, once produced, would not be accepted, loved, or nurtured by their parents and relatives. On the contrary, we freely admit that, like any child, they might be welcomed into the cloning family. Nevertheless, the cloned child's place in the scheme of family relations might well be uncertain and confused. The usually clear designations of father and brother, mother and sister, would be confounded. A mother could give birth to her own genetic twin, and a father could be genetically virtually identical to his son. The cloned child's relation to his or her grandparents would span one and two generations at once. . . .

The crucial point is not the *absence* of the natural biological connections between parents and children. The crucial point is, on the contrary, the *presence* of a unique, one-sided, and replicative biological connection to only *one* progenitor. As a result, family relations involving cloning would differ from all existing family arrangements, including those formed through adoption or with the aid of IVF. . . . Existing arrangements attempt in important ways to emulate the model of the natural family (at least in its arrangement of the generations), while cloning runs contrary to that model.

139

What the exact effects of cloning-to-produce-children might be for families is highly speculative, to be sure, but it is still worth flagging certain troubling possibilities and risks. . . . The problems of being and rearing an adolescent could become complicated should the teenage clone of the mother "reappear" as the double of the woman the father once fell in love with. Risks of competition, rivalry, jealousy, and parental tension could become heightened.

Cloned Children Would Seek Out "Originals"

Even if the child were cloned from someone who is not a member of the family in which the child is raised, the fact would remain that he or she has been produced in the nearly precise genetic image of another and for some particular reason, with some particular design in mind. Should this become known to the child, as most likely it would, a desire to seek out connection to the "original" could complicate his or her relation to the rearing family, as would living consciously "under the *reason*" for this extra-familial choice of progenitor. Though many people make light of the importance of biological kinship (compared to the bonds formed through rearing and experienced family life), many adopted children and children conceived by artificial insemination or IVF using donor sperm show by their actions that they do not agree. They make great efforts to locate their "biological parents," even where paternity consists in nothing more than the donation of sperm. Where the progenitor is a genetic near-twin, surely the urge of the cloned child to connect with the unknown "parent" would be still greater.

For all these reasons, the cloning family differs from the "natural family" or the "adoptive family." By breaking through the natural boundaries between generations, cloning could strain the social ties between them.

Effects on Society

The hazards and costs of cloning-to-produce-children may not be confined to the direct participants. The rest of society may also be at risk. The impact of human cloning on society at large may be the least appreciated, but among the most important, factors to consider in contemplating the morality of this activity.

Cloning is a human activity affecting not only those who are cloned or those who are clones, but also the entire society that allows or supports such activity. For insofar as the society *accepts* cloning-to-produce-children, to that extent the society may be said to *engage* in it. A society that allows dehumanizing practices—especially when given an opportunity to try to prevent them—risks becoming an accomplice in those practices. (The same could be said of a society that allowed even a few of its members to practice incest or polygamy.) Thus the question before us is whether cloning-to-produce-children is an activity that we, *as a society*, should engage in. In addressing this question, we must reach well beyond the rights of individuals and the difficulties or benefits that cloned children or their families might encounter. We must consider what kind of a society we wish to be. . . .

A society that clones human beings thinks about human beings (and especially children) differently than does a society that refuses to do so. It could easily be argued that we have already in myriad ways begun to show signs of regarding our children as projects on which we may work our wills. Further, it could be argued that we have been so desensitized by our earlier steps in this direction that we do not recognize this tendency as a corruption. While some people contend that cloning-to-produce-children would not take us much further down a path we have already been traveling, we would emphasize that the precedent of treating children as projects cuts two ways in the moral argument. Instead of using this precedent to justify taking the next step of cloning, the next step might rather serve as a warning and a mirror in which we may discover reasons to reconsider what we are already doing. Precisely because the stakes are so high, precisely because the new biotechnologies touch not only our bodies and minds but also the very idea of our humanity, we should ask ourselves how we as a society want to approach questions of human dignity and flourishing.

A Ban on Human Cloning Would Be Unconstitutional

Mark D. Eibert

Mark D. Eibert is an attorney who practices law in San Mateo, California. In the following selection he argues that laws banning reproductive cloning would be unconstitutional because the Supreme Court has ruled that every American has the right to make reproductive decisions without government interference. There are many infertile people who cannot have their own genetic children except, possibly, by means of cloning; to prohibit it would, in Eibert's opinion, deny them their right to reproduce. Furthermore, Eibert states that under the Constitution the government cannot decree that some children are too undesirable to be born. It would not even be permissible to prohibit cloning on grounds that it is unsafe, since parents are allowed to make their own decisions about other medical procedures that are risky for their unborn children.

Congress [has considered] "emergency" legislation to make it illegal for anyone to use cloning technology to have children. Proponents of such laws say they are justified by a long list of what they call "common American values." Before we outlaw an entire class of children, however, we should set aside the current hysteria, and rationally consider two "common American values" that are being overlooked: motherhood and reproductive freedom.

Why Would Anyone Want to Be "Cloned?"

Fifteen percent of Americans suffer from infertility, much of which cannot be cured by current medicine. For example, a

Consumer Reports study of fertility clinics showed that IVF [in vitro fertilization] and similar technologies work for only 25% of patients. That leaves *millions* of people who still cannot have children, often because they can't produce viable eggs or sperm, even with fertility drugs. Until now, their only options were to adopt, or to use eggs or sperm donated by strangers.

In a world blessed by cloning technology, however, viable eggs or sperm would not be needed to conceive children—any body cell would do. Thus, cloning offers infertile couples something everyone else takes for granted—the chance to have, raise and love their *own* genetic children.

With cloning, only one parent would contribute DNA, making the child almost a genetic twin. But America already has 1.5 million identical twins—and they are far from identical. They have different brain structures, IQ's, fingerprints and personalities, among other things.

Moreover, a child conceived by cloning would differ from her parent *much more* than identical twins differ from each other. The donor egg (which is necessary to cloning) would contribute about 5% of the child's genes. Also, the child would grow in a different uterus (which greatly affects fetal development), and be raised in a different family, decade and world.

In short, children conceived by cloning would not be "xerox copies" of anyone. They would be *babies* who would grow up to be *unique individuals*. That's what makes cloning attractive to millions of Americans who are otherwise unable to have their own genetic children. For them, cloning is about motherhood.

Cloning and the Constitution

The Supreme Court has ruled that every American has a constitutional right to "bear or beget" children, and to make reproductive decisions without government interference. This includes the right of infertile couples to use sophisticated medical technologies like IVF. As one court explained, "within the cluster of constitutionally protected choices that includes the right to have access to contraceptives, there must be included the right to submit to a medical procedure that may bring about, rather than prevent, pregnancy."

For many Americans, cloning technology, once perfected, will offer *the only way possible* to exercise their right to reproduce. As applied to them, cloning bans are the practical equivalent of forced sterilization. Yet, the Supreme Court struck down a law requiring the sterilization of convicted criminals, saying it violated "one of the fundamental rights of man." Surely, disabled citizens (as some courts classify infertile people) have at least as much right to have children as convicted rapists and child molesters.

There are also limits on government control over *who gets born*. Legislators cannot decree that *certain* children are too undesirable or imperfect to be born—that's an unconstitutional *eugenics law*, where the politicians play God.

In sum, a legal system where healthy Americans have a constitutional right to abort their children, but disabled Americans are barred from *conceiving* children, may appeal to many politicians, but it wouldn't survive its first trip to the courthouse.

Safety—or Pretext—First?

When the government tries to outlaw the exercise of a constitutional right—like having children—*it* has the burden of proving that the law is "necessary" to achieve a "compelling state interest" in the "least restrictive way" possible. If it fails, the courts declare the law unconstitutional.

Philosophical, religious and speculative concerns carry little or no legal weight. That leaves cloning opponents with only one weak argument—that at least in its current primitive state, cloning technology is not yet safe.

But the "safety" argument is a *pretext*—an excuse to outlaw something that politicians don't like for other reasons. The proposed laws contain no procedure for determining when cloning has become safe, or for lifting the ban once safety is achieved. Moreover, in a stroke of Orwellian genius, the proposed bans would *prevent* the very research and human clinical trials needed to *make* cloning safe.

Compare this with the treatment of other new medical procedures, hundreds of which are now in animal testing and not yet ready for safe human use. Nobody proposes to ban these treatments, or to discourage researchers from making them safe. Hardly any medical advance in history would have been legal if researchers had had to prove it safe for humans at the earliest stage of animal experimentation.

In addition, the "safety" argument ignores the issue of *who decides* how much risk is acceptable for a mother and her baby. In America, that decision is *always* made by the prospective parents, *never* by the government—not even where the potential harm is much more certain and serious than anything threatened by cloning. For example: IVF and fertility drugs are legal, even though they create higher risks of miscarriages, multiple births, and associated birth defects. (Indeed, the mother of the septuplets is considered a hero). Individuals with inheritable mental or physical defects, older mothers at risk of having babies with Downs Syndrome, and even AIDS mothers, are all allowed to reproduce, naturally and through IVF, even though they risk having babies with serious defects or illnesses. And although many states once had eugenics laws requiring the sterilization of retarded people (to prevent the birth of retarded children), such laws have long since been repealed or struck down.

The Real Question

Philosophers can speculate about the implications of cloning, but for politicians there is only one question: who should decide whether and how an individual can have children? The individual, or the government? Actually, it's a trick question. The Constitution permits only one answer.

Cloning Humans Is Not Yet Safe

Arlene Judith Klotzko

Arlene Judith Klotzko, a bioethicist and lawyer, is Writer in Residence at the Science Museum in London. She provides radio and TV commentary through the BBC and other news services, and has written or edited two books on cloning. In the following selection she expresses her belief that reproductive cloning is not wrong in principle, but is unsafe at present, and that it would be immoral to try it any time soon. As she points out, there have been abnormalities in the species cloned so far that resulted from the improper expression of genes—that is, whether the genes were turned on and off at the right time. This is because scientists do not yet understand the process of gene expression. In Klotzko's opinion, human reproductive cloning should not be attempted until they do.

As far as we know, human reproductive cloning has only been accomplished in fiction. Nevertheless, most people have strong moral views that using an ordinary body cell from someone who has already lived to reconstructing a new person would be wrong. Intrinsically wrong. I don't share that conviction. I believe that it would be immoral to clone a human being now or any time soon. It's simply unsafe.

Mammalian cloning burst upon the world stage in February 1997 in the form of a brash and very spoiled sheep named Dolly. Everyone was simply stunned. Just 13 years before, a consensus had emerged among developmental biologists that it was impossible to clone a mammal by nuclear transfer. In fact, Dolly was produced by just this process. Furthermore, by the end of 2003, a virtual Noah's arc—ten mammalian species—had been cloned, but not monkeys and, as far as anyone, knew, not humans. In February of [2004] came a stunning announcement from South Korea: Thirty human embryos had been cloned and one of them had yielded up its therapeutic treasure, human embryonic stem (ES) cells. [This report was later found to be untrue.] These are the master cells of our bodies. Capturing and directing their potential is one of the main goals of modern biological science.

Nuclear transfer is conceptually simple: Scientists remove the nucleus of an ordinary body cell—say a skin cell—and insert that nucleus into an egg whose nucleus has been removed. Substances left inside the egg cell then reprogramme the incoming nucleus, in effect, tricking it into having all the developmental potential of a one-cell embryo. In the UK, reproductive cloning is banned; therapeutic cloning is allowed, but only under a licence from the Human Fertilisation and Embryology Authority (HFEA).

Therapeutic Cloning Is Morally Acceptable

People disagree about the morality of cloning for cell therapies. I believe that the practice is morally acceptable and, because of the burden of incurable chronic disease that these therapies could alleviate, it is morally required. Even some who have no moral objections to therapeutic cloning oppose it in practice because of fears of the so-called slippery slope, an irrevocable slide to reproductive cloning. The basic idea behind such arguments is if you do x, which is morally acceptable, you will end up doing y (in our example, reproductive cloning) which is not. One can slide from x to y either because there is no way to distinguish between them conceptually or because the existence of x creates a social climate receptive to y. With our cloning example, neither of these conditions exists. Therapeutic cloning would be done to develop therapies for sick people, not to replicate them. And the availability of cell therapies would be utterly irrelevant to the permissibility of reproductive cloning.

Opponents of reproductive cloning often say that 'cloning is unnatural' or that 'scientists are playing God'. Such statements really don't get us anywhere. What is natural is not always benign. Think of infectious diseases, for example. Should we shun vaccines or antibiotics because they are not found in nature? What about spectacles [eye-glasses]? 'Playing God' evokes the horror inspired by Frankenstein creating life in the laboratory, but a visceral, instinctive shudder does not a moral argument make.

Moral Arguments Against Reproductive Cloning Are Speculative

Except for safety—more about this later—all of the moral arguments made against reproductive cloning are speculative. There are worries about strange family dynamics and the possibility of incest or incestuous feelings. There are concerns about a clone coming to believe that he or she would not have an open future medically or psychologically. Would a clone watch his father-twin become ill and thereby learn his own unavoidable destiny? If this were true, it would obviously be a grave burden. But it's not true. Even identical twins often don't develop the same diseases. Most diseases result from intricate interactions between genes, environment and lifestyle.

Would being a clone be psychologically harmful? Would a clone feel destined to repeat the choices and behaviours of his progenitor? No, I don't think so, at least not any more than might occur with children of high-achieving or famous parents.

Leon Kass, the chairman of President [George W.] Bush's Council on Bioethics, has written that cloning will lead to the commodification and devaluation of human beings. He said the same thing about IVF [in vitro fertilization] 25 years ago and his grim vision has not come to pass. In *Brave New World* [novelist Aldous] Huxley described the manufacture of babies by a combination of cloning and environmental conditioning. Kass fears that modern genetics will bring about just such a world. No law, no social consensus can prevent a slide into the abyss. I have more confidence in the law than he does, especially in [the U.K.]

Cloning Is Wrong Because It Is Unsafe

For me, the only moral objection to reproductive cloning that carries any weight is based on safety. There have been abnormalities—some horrific—in every mammalian species cloned thus far. The cause lies in the process of reprogramming that is at the heart of cloning. The defects result from improper or incomplete expression of genes (whether they are turned on and off at the right time). Because the problem is gene expression, rather than a mutation or defect, there is no screening test that can ensure a cloned embryo is normal. One day, we may fully understand the reprogramming process and be able to ensure it is done completely and correctly. That is certainly not possible at present. It is therefore morally irresponsible to attempt to produce a cloned human being—now and for the foreseeable future.

Identical Twins Are Natural Human Clones

Susan Reed

Susan Reed is a former editor of Time *magazine who is now a literary agent. In this selection she tells how different she and her sister are from each other even though they are identical twins. They are distinct individuals who share the same genes. They also shared the same womb and were raised in the same environment, which clones would not. Therefore, she says, clones would be even less alike than identical twins are. People who hoped that by cloning they could create a duplicate of someone they loved would be disappointed, and Reed feels that their expectations would create problems for the child.*

I have a clone. She lives in Pittsburgh, Pa., and her name is Diana. She's my body double: blond hair, hazel eyes and fair skin. She's half an inch taller, but we have the same voices and the same mannerisms. We're both unmarried. We love to read, we relish Mexican food, and we get the same patches of dry skin in winter. We both play tennis and golf. O.K., she's funnier than I am—but just a little.

In the debate over the ethical, emotional and practical implications of human cloning, identical twins—distinct beings who share the same DNA—present the closest analogy. Identical twins are in fact more similar to each other than a clone would be to his or her original, since twins gestate simultaneously in the same womb and are raised in the same environment at the same time, usually by the same parents.

But even with our genes and backgrounds the same, my sister and I are very different people. Diana is a corporate lawyer; I'm a former magazine editor, now a literary agent. She studied classics at Bryn Mawr; I studied the history of religion at Vassar. She favors clothes that have actual colors in them; I opt for black. She's politically conservative; I'm more liberal. She's a pragmatist; I'm an optimist.

We're not the only twins with differences in our family. My father, a writer and former diplomat, had an identical twin brother, Francis, who was a right-brained banker. Francis, who died in 1992, also had identical twin daughters. My cousin Rose is an intense adventurist while her sister Peg is softer and more traditional.

Of course, there are ways in which identical twins are bound together that are more profound than the usual sibling links. When I walk into a room, it takes no more than a glance before I can sense my twin's mood—if she's happy or tense or upset. I know what it's about and why. It's something I suspect few people, maybe not even all twins, experience. Would clones? I suspect not, since their life experiences would be so different.

Identical DNA Does Not Mean Identical People

Other connections between Diana and me may be more related to our matching DNA and thus more applicable to clones. My twin and I filter information in much the same way, and we think, perceive and interpret things similarly. When we're together, we often respond simultaneously with the same word or sentence. We have put on the same T shirt on the same day in different cities. We have friends who are twins, both doctors, who have similar experiences. They took a pharmacy class together in medical school but sat across the classroom from each other and took separate notes. They studied separately for the exam. When it was returned, they had missed the same questions, for the same reasons.

Despite these shared propensities, people who hope they can create a duplicate of, say, a lost child may be setting up that clone for heartbreak. Imagine the expectations that would be created for such a person. Comparisons are tough enough on identical twins. Between Diana and me, there were issues such as who got the better grade, who scored more points in a basketball game, who had more friends. But neither of us had to live with the idea that she was created to match up to the other's best features. A cloned child might not play the piano as well as the original. Or be as smart.

Identical twins are living proof that identical DNA doesn't mean identical people. My sister and I may have the same hardwiring—and a wire that connects us. We have fun with our similarities, but at the end of the day, there's no confusion about who is who. Just as the fingerprints of all individuals, even identical twins, are unique, so are their souls. And you can't clone a soul.

Human Clones Would Be Less Alike than Identical Twins

John Charles Kunich

John Charles Kunich is a professor of law at Roger Williams University. He is the author of two books, including, The Naked Clone: How Cloning Bans Threaten Our Personal Rights, *from which the following selection is taken. The book's title refers to the fact that potential children of cloning are "naked" in the legal sense, without any protection from laws that deprive them of the right to be born. Yet cloned people would not be fundamentally different from other people—they would be less alike than identical twins, who, as Kunich explains, are not really identical and share full legal rights with the rest of society. Clones would be years apart from their DNA donors in age, and would be born and grow up in different environments, making them true individuals. In Kunich's opinion, the means by which a child is brought into being has no relevance to that child's personhood, place in society, or legal rights.*

Some commentators have suggested that cloning is fundamentally different from "natural" procreation and even in vitro [outside the body] fertilization. This viewpoint holds that cloning is not reproduction but replication, akin to photocopying, and that the difference is of constitutional importance. Cloning has been excoriated as the moral and perhaps legal equivalent of slavery or incest. But these views reflect both a misunderstanding of cloning itself and an overemphasis on genotypic uniqueness as a prerequisite of personhood.

First, when the SCNT [somatic cell nuclear transfer] method is used, the mitochondrial DNA [m-DNA] is not

John Charles Kunich, *The Naked Clone: How Cloning Bans Threaten Our Personal Rights.* Westport, CT: Praeger, 2003. Copyright © 2003 by Greenwood Publishing Group, Inc. Reproduced by permission.

identical as between the donor of the nuclear DNA and the child of cloning. Their nuclear DNA will be the same, but their m-DNA will be different because the child of cloning will receive his or her m-DNA from the donor of the enucleated ovum. Thus, the two persons would not be truly identical genetically—extremely similar, but not identical. But even if there were absolute, 100 percent, genotypic identity between donor and child, it has never been deemed legally significant that two persons are genetically indistinguishable. All of us in fact have seen or met pairs of people who have exactly the same genetic codes, but these people were not children of cloning. They were "produced" through a much more ancient process.

Identical Twins Are Not Identical

Identical twins, or even identical siblings of more than two, are referred to as identical because they possess the same genotype. Because of a phenomenon occurring very early in the embryo's development, similar to the embryo-splitting method of cloning, a mother can give birth to two or more children with the same genetic structure and composition. Indeed, identical twins are more alike genetically than a DNA donor and his or her child of cloning because identical twins share the same m-DNA as well as the same nuclear DNA, and yet they are not identical in every aspect of their physical, mental, and behavioral characteristics.

For millennia, human identical twins have been born, lived their lives, and died. They were given individual names, nurtured as are other children, and afforded the same legal rights as all other people. True, identical twins may experience unusual parallels in their lives and life experiences, and they may enjoy particularly powerful relational bonds with one another, but they have not been denied full legal recognition of their personhood. Neither have they been found to lack individuality, dignity, or personal autonomy, despite some (undoubtedly well-intentioned parents) who dressed them alike, taught them alike, disciplined them alike, and continually expressed their expectations that they would fulfill parental expectations in like manner. They have generally managed to endure any teasing and joking, good-natured or otherwise, that was directed at them because of their two-of-a-kind situation.

Certainly, no one has argued that the genetic and environmental identity between identical twins is a reason they should not be allowed to exist. A search of the scholarly legal literature has failed to unearth any article asseverating that identical twins should be preemptively aborted because to allow them to be born would be tantamount to a wrongful life tort. Identical twins, with the identical nuclear DNA *and* the identical m-DNA, who share the same uterus at the same time, who are born within minutes of each other, and who grow up simultaneously in the identical home environment subject to the same parental pressures, are still universally viewed as having lives worth living. They may occasionally chafe at the influence of parents who want them to dress alike or who err on the side of excess in ensuring absolutely identical treatment for both twins in all things, but such are the types of annoyances that all children experience from their parents—no worse, only different. Some quantum of annoyance is the natural state of children with regard to their parents, and vice versa. It comes with the territory.

Identical Twins Lead Different Lives

Furthermore, there is certainly nothing identical about the way identical twins live their lives, despite some similarities. For millennia, identical twins have lived different life spans from one another, pursued different careers, contracted different diseases, and have had different experiences with such important life factors as sexual orientation, substance abuse, mental illness, and marriage. They did not appear to suffer from a crippling sense of diminished personal autonomy....

Identical Twins Feel a Bond

As in virtually all aspects of life in which human beings are involved, there is another side to the "problems" faced by identical twins. They may find a great measure of comfort, support, and fulfillment in the ineffable bond they feel to their identical sibling. Perhaps more than most sisters and brothers, they can enjoy a sense of true companionship with one another, an intangible emotional bridge that can span great expanses of time and space. This level of familial union, powerful enough to unite people throughout their lives with a special sense of shared essence, is something many nontwins would envy and covet in their own lives. Would donor and child of cloning enjoy a unique bond as well? Our experience with identical twins suggests that this is a real possibility.

The commentators who theorize that parents would feel and exhibit less emotional bonding to their children of cloning than to other children ignore the special bonds often felt between identical twins. One may safely presume that the majority of people interested in cloning would do so with one of three potential sources of DNA in mind: (1) themselves, (2) their life partner, or (3) their own child. In two of these three naked clone situations, a given parent would have a powerful genetic link to the child, and in the third, the child would possess a profound genetic link to a cherished loved one. Under all of these circumstances, if the evidence regarding identical twins is any indication, parents may feel a stronger emotional link to their children of cloning, not a weaker bond or a commodity-like detachment. These families may reasonably be expected to enjoy a higher level of emotional bonding, greater mutual solicitude, and deeper shared understanding—far from the feared "despotism of the cloners over the cloned," a reversion to the cruel practices of ancient Sparta, and the depersonalized treatment of children as "artifacts" or "products."

Clones Would Be Less Alike than Twins

The genotypic identity between DNA donor and child of cloning is properly viewed in the same light as identical twins, with, if anything, even more powerful arguments in support of personhood and individuality. As with identical twins, there may eventuate striking similarities in certain aspects of life, but also important differences. Unlike identical twins, the donor and child of cloning would be some years apart in age, often a generation or more apart, with all the cultural and experiential divergences that implies. In all circumstances except the situation in which parents seek to clone their own child, the donor and child of cloning would have different parents, would be carried in different uteri, and would be raised in a different household environment.

The DNA donor and the child of cloning would have different friends and close relatives, would have different teachers, and would be shaped by many divergent environmental factors. They may prefer quite different diets, and the foods they eat, both in terms of type and quantity, would exert a major influence on their appearance, health, lifestyle habits, and longevity. They could have divergent attitudes to such significant life-shaping activities as exercise, nutrition, and proper rest, as well as potentially harmful tobacco use, alcohol consumption, and use of illegal drugs. They may well be more dissimilar than identical twins reared apart.

The fact that DNA donor and the child of cloning have m-DNA from completely different sources also would have a considerable influence on the degree of similarity between the two people. Differences would be expected "in parts of the body that have high demands for energy—such as muscle, heart, eye, and brain—or in body systems that use mitochondrial control over cell death to determine cell numbers." But irrespective of how similar they may be in terms of genotype, phenotype, personality, and preferences, they would be every bit as much individual persons as are identical twins, under the law. Any attempt to elide cloning with mechanical replication would not be capable of formulating a legally significant deficiency in the naked clone.

Rearing Would Not Make Clones into Copies

This is true despite possible parental exertions to rear the child of cloning to be the living replacement of a particular individual or a faithful replica of a living exemplar. Under some of the scenarios envisioned, a person or couple might want to clone in order to give a dying loved one "another chance," or to honor and emulate an admired person, even oneself. In these situations, the caregivers could be expected to make every effort to bring up the new child in the same manner as the DNA donor. They might supply the same bedroom, toys, books, music, clothing, games, lessons, and videos. They could try to re-create many of the same cherished life experiences, such as favorite vacations, outings, activities, and educational opportunities. They might try to narrow the range of options and experiences open to the child. In short, they may do everything that countless legions of parents have done throughout the ages in an attempt to live vicariously through their children and to have them carry on the family business and traditions. And they (and their children) may be just as surprised, pleased, and/or frustrated by the results, just as monozygotic twins can look and act very different from one another, notwithstanding the efforts of parents to make them alike in every way.

The same is true for parents who choose to clone in the hope that their child will display outstanding talents in some-selected areas of endeavor. Whether their objective is a super-star baseball player, a musical prodigy, a mathematical wizard, or a scientific genius, people who selectively clone on the basis of guaranteeing success in a specific area would understandably choose a willing DNA donor whose phenotype and achievements they consider optimal under all the circumstances. Once they secure the best available DNA for their child's genotype, they would rear the child with great emphasis on education, training, exposure, and experience in the chosen field, immersing the child in the subject matter. And again, the results will be as unpredictable (or as predictably diverse) as those obtained by countless other well-meaning but overbearing parents throughout human history. Certainly and inevitably, some parents will be disappointed with the behavior and achievements of their children of cloning in these situations, and the children will be aware of some degree of parental disapproval. But to suggest that this is anything new, or that it would be immeasurably worse than it has been for children and parents from time immemorial, is rank speculation at best.

Because human beings are not sheep, literally or figuratively (with apologies to Dolly), free will is a vital and often unpredictable variable in every life. Regardless of a person's genotype, he or she has the freedom to exercise individual options across a sprawling spectrum of life choices, year by year. Even the staunchest exponents of genetic determinism would admit that there is something ineffable about being human, something that surpasses genetic makeup. If the courts that will grapple with anticloning legislation grasp this, they will inexorably be drawn to the conclusion that SCNT cloning is properly analyzed as another form of human reproduction, different from the others not in the fundamentals but only in the details. . . .

Cloning Is Not Mass Production

The extreme slippery-slope horrors conjured up by some opponents of cloning contain even less substance. As previously pointed out, cloning has nothing to do with mass-production of identical people. Whether the feared outcome is an army of Adolf Hitlers, a *fatwa* spearheaded by thousands of Osama bin Ladens, an NBA overflowing with Michael Jordans, or a Las Vegas showroom full of Elvis Presleys, the fears are unfounded—the stuff of nightmares or pipe dreams. Cloning cannot be carried out in a factory arrayed with row upon row of large test tubes, despite various depictions in popular films such as the *Jurassic Park* series. Every embryo would need to be individually implanted in the uterus of a living woman, one per person, and gestated for the usual nine months, with all the inconveniences, travails, discomfort, and pain that has always entailed.

In addition, it is important to remember that the outcome obtained after all of those failed attempts and after nine months of gestation is a human baby. Cloning does not "produce" a full-formed adult creature such as Frankenstein's monster, ready off-the-shelf to wreak havoc on an unsuspecting world. When any living creature is born through the intervention of cloning, that creature is a human baby, needing to be fed and changed and constantly cared for. The personality, powers, and predilections that will be exhibited by that baby as an adult will not be evident for many years, just as with all other human babies. Thus, anyone who expects to use cloning to create adults for any specific aim, whether benign or evil, would have to be exceedingly patient and ready to work and wait for decades for the eventual result. Will any mad scientist or archvillain be willing or able to change diapers, breast-feed, and burp the hoped-for army of future henchmen in their infancy? . . .

Clones Would Be Entitled to Legal Protection

Once we move beyond the horror-movie level of argument, the anti-cloning position remains equally unpersuasive. Is there a realistic possibility that children of cloning will be enslaved, used as involuntary organ donors, treated as commodties, or otherwise disproportionately be abused and depersonialized? Will their caregivers consider them subhuman, more akin to property or pets than children, and subject them to a phalanx of physical and psychological assaults? Will families dissolve as parents, having exercised total control over their children's genotypes, somehow feel less emotional attachment to them, feeling no more bond to them than to their cars or sweaters or any other manufactured product? . . .

There is no question that children born through cloning would be entitled to every legal protection applicable to all other children. There is absolutely no danger that these children would somehow be exempted from the laws prohibiting child abuse, mandating proper care and support of children, requiring the education of children, outlawing the non-consensual harvesting of organs, and banning child labor and involuntary servitude. These laws would be fully applicable and would stand as a deterrent to would-be violators with the same efficacy as in all other circumstances.

Human Clones Would Be Treated as If They Were Exact Copies

Søren Holm

Søren Holm is a law school professor at Cardiff University in Wales, where he teaches bioethics at the Cardiff Institute for Society, Health and Ethics. He is the director of the Cardiff Centre for Ethics, Law, and Society. In the following selection he argues that although it is not true that cloned persons would be identical copies of their DNA donors or that genes determine personality, the public nevertheless believes these misconceptions. Therefore, a cloned child would be expected to be an exact copy and would be forced to live his or her life in the shadow of someone else. For this reason, Holm believes that human cloning should not be allowed.

One of the arguments which is often put forward in the discussion of human cloning is that it is in itself wrong to create a copy of a human being. This argument is usually dismissed by pointing out that (a) we do not find anything wrong in the existence of monozygotic twins even though they are genetically identical, and (b) the clone would not be an exact copy of the original, even in those cases where it is an exact genetic copy, since it would experience a different environment which would modify its biological and psychological development (throughout, . . . I will assume that clones are perfect genetic copies, even though the present cloning techniques do not in most instances produce perfect clones because they do not clone the mitochondrial DNA).

In my view both these counterarguments are valid, but nevertheless I think that there is some core of truth in the assertion that it is wrong deliberately to try to create a copy of an already existing human being. It is this idea which I will briefly try to explicate here.

The Life-in-the-Shadow Argument

When we see a pair of monozygotic twins [twins from one fertilized egg] who are perfectly identically dressed some of us experience a slight sense of unease, especially in the cases where the twins are young children. This unease is exacerbated in cases where people establish competitions where the winners are the most identical pair of twins. The reason for this uneasiness is, I believe, that the identical clothes could signal a reluctance on the part of the parents to let each twin develop his or her individual and separate personality or a reluctance to let each twin lead his or her own life. In the extreme case each twin is constantly compared with the other and any difference is counteracted.

In the case of cloning based on somatic cells we have what is effectively a set of monozygotic twins with a potentially very large age difference. The original may have lived all his or her life and may even have died before the clone is brought into existence. One of the scenarios where cloning might be desired is in a family in which a child is dying or has died, and the parents wish to replace this child with a child who is genetically identical. In such a case there would not be any direct day-by-day comparison or identical clothing, but I think that a situation even worse for the clone is likely to develop. I shall call this situation "a life in the shadow," and I shall develop an argument against human cloning that may be labeled the "life in the shadow argument."

Let us try to imagine what will happen when a clone is born and its social parents begin rearing it. Usually when a child is born we ask hypothetical questions like "How will it develop?" or "What kind of person will it become?" and we often answer them with reference to various psychological traits we think we can identify in the biological mother or father or in their families, for instance "I hope that he won't get the kind of temper you had when you were a child!"

The Public Assumes Genes Determine Personality

In the case of the clone, however, we are likely to give much more specific answers to such questions. Answers that will then go on to affect the way the child is reared. There is no doubt that the common public understanding of the relationship between genetics and psychology contains substantial strands of genetic essentialism, that is, the idea that genes determine psychology and personality. This public idea is reinforced every time the media report the findings of new genes for depression, schizophrenia, and every time a novel or a film portrays a link between the "criminal traits" of an adopted child and the psychology of its biological parents. Therefore it is likely that the parents of the clone will already have formed in their minds a quite definite picture of how the clone will develop, a picture based on the actual development of the original. This picture will control the way they rear the child. They will try to prevent some developments and promote others. Just imagine how a clone of Adolf Hitler or [murderous Cambodian dictator] Pol Pot would be reared or how a clone of Albert Einstein, Ludwig van Beethoven, or Michael Jordan would be brought up. The clone would in a very literal way live his or her life in the shadow of the life of the original. At every point in the clone's life there would be someone who had already lived that life, with whom the clone could be compared and against whom the clone's accomplishments could be measured.

That there would in fact be a strong tendency to make the inference from genotype to phenotype and to let the conclusion of such an inference affect rearing can perhaps be seen more clearly if we imagine a hypothetical situation. Suppose that in the future new genetic research reveals that there are only a limited number of possible human genotypes, and that genotypes are therefore recycled every 300 years (i.e., somebody who died 300 years ago had exactly the same genotype that I have). It is further discovered that there is some complicated, but not practically impossible, method whereby it is possible to discover the identity of the persons who 300, 600, 900, and so on years ago instantiated the genotype which a specific fetus now has. I am absolutely certain that people would split in two sharply disagreeing camps if this became a possibility. One group, perhaps the majority, would try to identify the previous instantiations of their child's genotype. Another group would emphatically not seek this information because they would not want to know and would not want their children to grow up in the shadow of a number of previously led lifes with the same genotype. The option to remain in ignorance is not open, however, to social parents of contemporary clones.

If the majority would seek the information in this scenario, firms offering the method of identification would have a very brisk business, and it could perhaps even become usual to expect of prospective parents that they made use of this new possibility. Why would this happen? The only reasonable explanation, apart from initial curiosity, is that people would believe that by identifying the previous instantiation of the genotype they would thereby gain valuable knowledge about their child. But knowledge is in general only valuable if it can be converted into new options for action, and the most likely form of action would be, that information about the previous instantiations would be used in deciding how to rear the present child. This again points to the importance of the public perception of genetic essentialism, since the environment must have changed considerably in the 300-year span between each instantiation of the genotype.

What Is Wrong About a Life in the Shadow?

But what is wrong with living your life as a clone in the shadow of the life of the original? It seems to me that it diminishes the clone's possibility of living a life which is in a full sense of that word *his* or *her* life. The clone is forced to be involved in an attempt to perform a complicated partial reenactment of the life of somebody else. In our usual arguments for the importance of respect for autonomy or for the value of self-determination we often affirm that it is the final moral basis for these principles, that they enable persons to live their lives the way they themselves want to live these lives. If we deny part of this opportunity to clones and force them to live their lives in the shadow of someone else we are violating some of our most fundamental moral principles and intuitions. Therefore, as long as genetic essentialism is a common cultural belief there are good reasons not to allow human cloning.

It is important to note that the life-in-the-shadow argument does not rely on the false premise that we can make an inference from genotype to (psychological or personality) phenotype, but only on the true premise that there is a strong public tendency to make such an inference. This means that the conclusions of the argument follow only as long as this empirical premise remains true. If ever the public relinquishes all belief in genetic essentialism the life-in-the-shadow argument would fail, but such a development seems highly unlikely. It could be suggested that the argument does not speak against cloning, but for a much more active information campaign to change people's erroneous beliefs in genetic essentialism. This is absolutely correct, but there are two important things to note about this suggestion. The first is that it is probably unrealistic to expect much change in public perceptions about genetics, even if we mount a very strong information campaign. The beliefs concerning the relationship between "blood" and character traits are culturally very old and deeply entrenched in our way of thinking. We may therefore never reach a situation where the life-in-the-shadow scenario disappears. Second a belief in genetic essentialism is definitely wrong, but it is not in itself inherently ethically problematic, as is, for instance, a belief in the natural superiority of one specific race. It is thus not certain that we can draw an analogy from the sound argument that the negative consequences of racist beliefs should be combated by changing the beliefs not by accommodating them, to a similar argument about beliefs in genetic essentialism.

Response to Counterarguments

In conclusion I should perhaps also mention that I am fully aware of two possible counterarguments to the argument presented above. The first points out that even if a life in the shadow of the original is perhaps problematic and not very good, it is the only life the clone can have, and that it is therefore in the clone's interest to have this life as long as it is not worse than having no life at all. The life-in-the-shadow argument therefore does not show that cloning should be prohibited. I am unconvinced by this counterargument, just as I am by all arguments involving comparisons between existence and nonexistence, but it is outside the scope of this [discussion] to show decisively that the counterargument is wrong. It is, however, perhaps worth noting that if the argument is accepted it also entails that every kind of intervention I perform which in some way harms a future human person is ethically innocuous, as long as I make sure that either (a) it is part of a series of interventions leading to the only life the person can have, or (b) make sure that the intervention harms the embryo, fetus, or newborn sufficiently for it to become a different person from the one it would have been without the intervention (thereby ensuring the fulfillment of criterion (a)). I find this conclusion profoundly counterintuitive and morally pernicious.

The second counterargument states that the conclusions of the life-in-the-shadow argument can be avoided if all clones are anonymously put up for adoption, so that no knowledge about the original is available to the social parents of the clone. I am happy to accept this counterargument, but I think that a system where I was not allowed to rear the clone of myself would practically annihilate any interest in human cloning. The attraction in cloning for many is exactly in the belief that a person can re-create himself. The cases in which human cloning might solve real medical or reproductive problems are on the fringe.

Human Cloning Would Lead to a Loss of Empathy

Jeremy Rifkin

Jeremy Rifkin is the president of the Foundation on Economic Trends, a private foundation based in Washington, D.C., that examines emerging trends in science and technology and their impacts on the environment, the economy, culture, and society. He is the author of many books on these subjects. In the following selection Rifkin argues that cloning humans would ultimately have a bad effect on the way people relate to each other. Children have traditionally been viewed as unique creations of God or nature; but, he says, cloned babies would be thought of in terms of quality controls and predictable outcome. In Rifkin's opinion, this would lead to the production of "designer babies," a step beyond cloning in which a child's genes are customized. How then, he asks, would society regard those children who are not customized? They might be considered defective, and if so, Rifkin says, future generations would expect perfection in their offspring and would lose the human capacity to empathize with people who are not perfect.

Our species stands at a great divide. Before us lies the imminent prospect of the cloning of a human being. With this feat, we play God with our evolutionary destiny, and risk ominous consequences for the future of civilisation. Already researchers are readying the first experiments and the world anxiously awaits this "second coming"—except this time the child will have been produced by science and in the image of a specific human being.

This scares many people but, proponents argue, why not? If, for example, an infertile couple desires to pass on their genetic inheritance by producing clones of one or both partners, shouldn't they be able to exercise their right of choice? Moreover, we are told not to be overly concerned because even though the clone will have the exact same genetic makeup as the original, he or she will develop differently because the social and environmental context within which his or her life unfolds will not be the same as the donor.

Some professional ethicists, on the other hand, shake their heads and mutter about the yuck factor—people's initial disgust at the prospect of cloning a human being—but when pressed, can offer few, if any, compelling reasons to oppose what they consider to be inevitable and even worthwhile, under certain circumstances. Their only misgivings appear to be whether or not the procedure is safe and whether the baby would be malformed. Right to life advocates worry, in turn, that embryos used in the procedure will be wasted or discarded in attempts to produce a successful clone. Unfortunately, the deeper issues surrounding the cloning of a human being have received short shrift or no attention at all.

Cloning Will Have a Major Effect on Human History

The cloning of a human raises fundamental questions that go to the very nature of what it means to be a human being. No other single event in human history will have had as great an effect on the future of our species. Here are the reasons why. To begin with, our very notion of what life is all about is immersed in sexuality and the biological attraction of male and female. Much of the history of civilisation has played out along sexual lines, from mating rituals to the notions of family, clan, tribe and nation. From time immemorial we have thought of the birth of our progeny as a gift bestowed by God and or a beneficent nature. The coming together of sperm and egg represents a moment of surrender to forces outside of our control. The fusing of maleness and femaleness results in a unique and finite new creation.

The reason most people have an almost instinctual repulsion to cloning is that deep down, they sense that it signals the beginning of a new journey where the "gift of life" is steadily marginalised and eventually abandoned all together. In its place, the new progeny becomes the ultimate shopping experience—designed in advance, produced to specification and purchased in the biological marketplace.

Cloning is, first and foremost, an act of "production", not creation. Using the new biotechnologies, a living being is produced with the same degree of engineering as we have come to expect on an assembly line. When we think of engineering standards, what immediately comes to mind is quality controls and predictable outcomes. That's exactly what cloning a human being is all about. For the first time in the history of our species, we can dictate the final genetic constitution of the offspring. The child is no longer a unique creation—one of a kind—but rather a reproduction. Human cloning opens the door wide to the dawn of a commercial eugenics civilisation, a brave new world where new technologies speed the process of "improving" our offspring, allowing us to create a second genesis. This time, each person can become a private god and make offspring in his or her own image.

Cloning Will Lead to Designer Babies

In the future—certainly by the time today's babies reach adulthood—it will be possible to make genetic changes in the donor cell or embryo and begin creating customised variations of the original. Ian Wilmut, of the Roslin Institute, near Edinburgh, has already accomplished this feat in his second cloned sheep. Though less celebrated than Dolly, the birth of Polly is far more ominous. With Polly, Wilmut's team customised a human gene into a sheep cell and then cloned the sheep, making it the first truly "designer animal". Using the clone as a "standard model", scientists can now produce endless customised variations suited to the requisites of their clients.

Does anyone doubt for a moment that what Wilmut accomplished with Polly won't be made available by the biotech industry to parents who would like to produce cloned designer babies? Again, proponents argue, why not? If a prospective parent knew they were likely to pass on a genetic predisposition for heart disease, or stroke, or cancer, wouldn't they feel obligated to spare their clone by eliminating those genes in the donor cell or embryo? But where does one draw the line? What if the parent knew he or she was likely to pass on a genetic predisposition for bipolar manic depression, or dyslexia, or growth hormone deficiency, or a cleft palate? Doesn't every parent want the best possible life for their child? In the future, some would argue, parental responsibility and intervention ought to begin at the design stage, in the donor cell or cloned embryo.

Customised human cloning offers the spectre of a new kind of immortality. Each generation of a particular genotype can become the ultimate artist, continually customising and upgrading new genetic traits into the model with the goal of both perfecting and perpetuating the genotype forever. It would be naive to believe that there aren't lots of people who would leap at the opportunity. Researchers at fertility clinics say that they are already besieged by requests to clone.

Will Uncustomized Children Be Called Defective?

The real threat that human cloning represents is one that, as far as I know, is never talked about by scientists, ethicists, biotech entrepreneurs, or politicians. In a society where more and more people clone and eventually customise their genotype to design specifications and engineering standards, how are we likely to regard the child who isn't cloned or customised? What about the child who is born with a "disability"? Will the rest of society view that child with tolerance or come to see the child as an error in the genetic code—in short a defective product? Indeed, future generations might become far less tolerant of those who are not engineered and who deviate from the genetic standards and norms adhered to in the "best practices" of the bioindustrial marketplace. If that were to happen, we might lose the most precious gift of all, the human capacity to empathise with each other. When we empathise with another human being, it's because we feel and experience their vulnerability, their frailties and suffering, and their unique struggle to claim their humanity. But, in a world that comes to expect perfection in its offspring, can empathy really survive?

Human cloning represents the ultimate Faustian bargain. In our desire to become the architects of our own evolution, we risk the very real possibility of losing our humanity.

Negative Attitudes Toward Human Clones Would Be Discrimination

Julian Savulescu

Julian Savulescu is a professor of philosophy at Oxford University in England and the director of the Oxford Uehiro Centre for Practical Ethics. In the following selection, he explains why he does not believe the arguments put forth by opponents of human cloning are valid. In Savulescu's opinion, attitudes that had a negative effect on the lives of clones would be a new form of discrimation against a group of humans who were perceived as different. Misinformed bigotry, he says, is not a reason to prevent cloning—it is a reason to change the attitudes. He argues that society should protect clones from the results of prejudice, just as it protects other minorities.

The first reproductive clone of a human being will inevitably arrive at some time in the future. The first human clone will be the first 'artificial' human, the first true 'test-tube baby' to be created by science, made in a way utterly different to what God or nature ordained for us.

Reproductive cloning could allow new and important options for people with mitochondrial disease, and couples where the male partner has no viable sperm, to create a child genetically related to themselves. IVF [in vitro fertilization] couples producing a small number of embryos could also take cells from their embryos (or fetuses) for cloning, to increase the number of available embryos, in case a pregnancy fails. Cloning could produce an embryo, or help create a child, to be a donor of stem cells for a sick sibling or relative. Cloning will become just another reproductive technique, along with sexual reproduction and IVF.

Reasons for Opposing Cloning Are Not Valid

Of course, many people currently oppose even therapeutic cloning, because of fears of slipping down the slope to reproductive cloning. But what are the reasons to oppose reproductive cloning? When Dolly the sheep was cloned, the German Prime Minister said this would lead to 'xeroxing people'. But the current techniques of cloning could not clone or copy people. They copy a genome, a person's complete DNA sequence. Only a crude genetic determinist could claim that cloning copies people. The DNA of Hitler, Einstein or Mozart in their clones would never produce Hitler, Einstein or Mozart. We are the product of our genes, but also our environment and most importantly, our own free choices.

The European Parliament, UNESCO [United Nations Educational Scientific and Cultural Organization] and WHO [Word Health Organization] all state that reproductive cloning is an 'affront to human dignity'. But identical twins—natural clones—occur at a rate of about 3 per 1000 births. In the past, twins were seen as evil and killed at birth, their existence an affront to human dignity. But today, we see identical twins as ordinary and autonomous individuals. No one is developing drugs to reduce the rate of identical twinning because it is an affront to human dignity, or because it is so terrible to live one's life as a twin.

Some clones would be different to twins, in that the clone might be a copy of a genome of an already-existing person. Accordingly, the European Parliament pronounced that 'the individual has a right to his or her own genetic identity'. But where does a 'right to genetic individuality' come from? It is hard to see the value of 'genetic individuality' especially where an embryo or baby dying very early in life was then cloned. Or, where the person who was cloned is long dead or living in a different country. A clone of that embryo or person being raised by another family would be more like an identical twin being reared apart from its sibling.

Clonism: A New Form of Discrimination

But might some clones 'live in the shadow' of the earlier clone, exposed to the expectations and biases people might have from knowing the older clone, closing the new cloned child's future? [Philosopher David] Oderberg writes of 'identity confusion' and 'unbearable expectations placed on the child's shoulder's. Rather, in my view, what would make clones' lives problematic is the way in which their parents, peers and society might treat them. Negative attitudes towards clones would be a new form of discrimination—clonism—against a group of humans who are different in a non-morally significant way. To say that creating a clone is an affront to human dignity is like saying that deliberately creating a black person, or a woman, affronts human dignity. The statement itself affronts the dignity of cloned people. Misinformed bigotry is not a reason to prevent cloning, rather a reason to drop the attitudes.

Parents already create families for all kinds of private reasons, in a variety of ways, with and without medical assistance. The role of the cloned child's parents would be the same as all of these parents': to love the child and give it a good upbringing. Whether clones have good or bad lives simply depends on society and how we choose to treat them, not on the facts of their DNA. We should not fear cloning technology, but instead should use it rationally and responsibly. And we should continue to treat other people, including clones, when they arrive, with equal concern and respect, making sure others also do the same.

Cloning is currently unsafe and [Severino] Antinori [an Italian doctor who claimed to have cloned a child] is playing Russian Roulette. But if reproductive cloning were in the future to become safe and successful, or if we attempt cloning by embryo splitting, there would be no moral reason to ban cloning by law. Morality should be about people and their lives—not about any other individual's feelings of repugnance about them. As we speak up for those affected by racism, sexism, homophobia—so we should protect future clones in society. We have nothing to fear from cloning or biological modification of human beings except ourselves.

Organizations to Contact

Americans to Ban Cloning (ABC)
1100 H St. NW, Suite 700
  Washington, DC 20005
(202) 347-6840 • fax: (202) 347-6849
e-mail: media@cloninginformation.org
Web site: www.cloninginformation.org

The Americans to Ban Cloning coalition is a group of concerned Americans and U.S.-based organizations that promote a global, comprehensive ban on human cloning. Its Web site contains commentary, congressional testimony, and news.

Biotechnology Industry Organization (BIO)
1225 St. NW, Suite 400
  Washington, DC 20005
(202) 962-9200
e-mail: info@bio.org
Web sites: www.bio.org and http://science.bio.org

BIO is a trade and lobbying organization for the biotechnology industry, representing companies and academic institutions. It aims to be the champion of biotechnology and the advocate for its member organizations. Its Web sites contain information about the benefits of cloning.

Center for Bioethics and Human Dignity
2065 Half Day Rd.
  Bannockburn, IL 60015
(847) 317-8180 • fax: (847) 317-8101
e-mail: info@cbhd.org
Web site: www.cbhd.org

The Center for Bioethics and Human Dignity is a nonprofit organization that exists to help individuals and organizations address pressing bioethical challenges, including managed care, end-of-life treatment, genetic intervention, euthanasia and suicide, and reproductive technologies. It advocates banning both reproductive and therapeutic cloning.

Center for Genetics and Society
436 Fourteenth St., Suite 700
Oakland, CA 94612
(510) 625-0819 • fax: (510) 625-0874
Web site: www.genetics-and-society.org

The Center for Genetics and Society is a nonprofit information and public affairs organization working to encourage responsible uses and effective societal governance of human genetic and reproductive technologies. It works with a network of scientists, health professionals, civil society leaders, and others. Its Web site contains a large amount of informational material.

Coalition for the Advancement of Medical Research (CAMR)
2021 K St. NW, Suite 305
Washington, DC 20006
(202) 293-2856
e-mail: CAMResearch@yahoo.com
Web site: www.stemcellfunding.org

The Coalition for the Advancement of Medical Research is comprised of nationally recognized patient organizations, universities, scientific societies, foundations, and individuals with life-threatening illnesses and disorders, advocating for the advancement of breakthrough research and technologies in regenerative medicine in order to cure disease and alleviate suffering. It aims to ensure that somatic cell nuclear transfer (SCNT), also known as therapeutic cloning, remains a legal and viable form of scientific research, but it opposes any effort that would allow reproductive cloning.

Council for Responsible Genetics (CRG)
5 Upland Rd., Suite 3
Cambridge, MA 02140
(617) 868-0870 • fax: (617) 491-5344
e-mail: crg@gene-watch.org
Web site: www.gene-watch.org

The Council for Responsible Genetics is a nonprofit, nongovernmental organization that fosters public debate about the social, ethical, and environmental implications of genetic technologies. It is strongly opposed to human reproductive cloning. It publishes a bimonthly magazine, *GeneWatch*, of which partial archives can be found at its Web site.

Genetics Policy Institute (GPI)

11924 Forest Hill Blvd., Suite 22
Wellington, FL 33414-6258
(888) 238-1423 • fax: (561) 791-3889
Web site: www.genpol.org

The Genetics Policy Institute is a leading nonprofit organization dedicated to establishing a positive legal framework to advance the search for cutting-edge cures. It serves as a unifying voice for patients, researchers, universities and nonprofit organizations throughout the world in calling upon legislative bodies to ban reproductive cloning while preserving scientific freedom in the pursuit of cures through somatic cell nuclear transfer (SCNT).

Genetic Savings & Clone

(888) 833-6063 • fax: (415) 289-2526
Web site: www.savingsandclone.com

Genetic Savings & Clone is a commercial company that offers cloning of cats and hopes to eventually clone dogs. Its Web site contains extensive information about the technology and ethics of pet cloning, including pictures of the cats that have been cloned so far. It also maintains a site at www. DefendPetCloning.org, a direct response to NoPetCloning.org, which opposes cloning.

Hastings Center

21 Malcolm Gordon Rd.
Garrison, NY 10524-5555
(845) 424-4040 • fax: (845) 424-4545
e-mail: mail@thehastingscenter.org
Web site: www.thehastingscenter.org

The Hastings Center is an independent, nonpartisan, and nonprofit bioethics research institute that explores fundamental and emerging questions in health care, biotechnology, and the environment. It publishes the bimonthly *Hastings Center Report*, which includes essays, commentary, and scholarly articles, as well as many books and papers.

Human Cloning Foundation (HCF)
e-mail: contactus@humancloning.org
Web site: www.humancloning.org

The nonprofit Human Cloning Foundation exists to promote human cloning and other forms of biotechnology. It believes that cloning technology can be used to cure diseases, prolong life, and cure infertility. Its Web site contains many pro-cloning essays and a message board, which is its preferred method of contact.

NoPetCloning.org
801 Old York Rd., #204
   Jenkintown, PA 19046
(215) 887-0816 • fax: (215) 887-2088
e-mail: info@nopetcloning.org
Web site: www.nopetcloning.org

A Web site created by the American Anti-Vivisection Society to educate the public about the dangers it believes are inherent in pet cloning.

President's Council on Bioethics
1801 Pennsylvania Ave. NW, Suite 700
   Washington, DC 20006
(202) 296-4669
e-mail: info@bioethics.gov
Web site: www.bioethics.gov

This council advises the president of the United States on ethical issues related to advances in biomedical science and technology. Its reports, some of which are book length, are available at the site.

Reproductive Cloning Network (RCN)
506 Hudson St., New York, NY 10014
(212) 255-1439 12
e-mail: rhwicker@optonline.net
Web site: www.reproductivecloning.net

The principal objective of the Reproductive Cloning Network is to provide those interested in the underlying science of reproductive cloning with fundamental information, scientific statistics, and links to the relevant organizations and companies. It is affiliated with the Human Cloning Foundation.

Roslin Institute
Roslin BioCentre, Midlothian EH25 9PS
    Scotland, UK
Web site: www.roslin.ak.uk

The Roslin Institute is the scientific institution that cloned Dolly the sheep. Its site offers educational information for the general public about animal cloning.

Student Society for Stem Cell Research (SSSCR)
303 Bannockburn Ave., Tampa, FL 33617
e-mail: info@ssscr.org
Web site: www.ssscr.org

The Student Society for Stem Cell Research is an international body of students who believe that stem cell research will revolutionize the field of medicine. It is a sponsored project of the Genetic Policy Institute.

Bibliography

Books

Ronald Bailey	*Liberation Biology: The Scientific and Moral Case for the Biotech Revolution.* Amherst, NY: Prometheus Books, 2005.
Andrea L. Bonnicksen	*Crafting a Cloning Policy: From Dolly to Stem Cells.* Washington, DC: Georgetown University Press, 2002.
Michael C. Brannigan, ed.	*Ethical Issues in Human Cloning: Cross-Disciplinary Perspectives.* New York: Seven Bridges Press, 2001.
Elaine Dewar	*The Second Tree: Stem Cells, Clones, Chimeras, and Quests for Immortality.* New York: Carroll & Graf, 2004.
Karl Drlica	*Understanding DNA and Gene Cloning: A Guide for the Curious.* Hoboken, NJ: Wiley, 2004.
Jay D. Gralla and Preston Gralla	*The Complete Idiot's Guide to Understanding Cloning.* New York: Alpha Books, 2004.
John Harris	*On Cloning.* New York: Routledge, 2004.
Arlene Judith Klotzko	*A Clone of Your Own.* New York: Cambridge University Press, 2005.
Arlene Judith Klotzko, ed.	*The Cloning Sourcebook.* New York: Oxford University Press, 2003.

Francis Fukuyama   *Our Posthuman Future: Consequences of the Biotechnology Revolution.* New York: Farrar, Straus & Giroux, 2002.

Leon R. Kass   *Life, Liberty, and the Defense of Dignity: The Challenge for Bioethics.* San Francisco: Encounter Books, 2002.

William Kristol and Eric Cohen, eds.   *The Future Is Now: America Confronts the New Genetics.* Lanham, MD: Rowman & Littlefield, 2002.

John Charles Kunich   *The Naked Clone: How Cloning Bans Threaten Our Personal Rights.* Westport, CT: Praeger, 2003.

Stephen E. Levick   *Clone Being: Exploring the Psychological and Social Dimensions.* Lanham, MD: Rowman & Littlefield, 2004.

Kerry Lynn Macintosh   *Illegal Beings: Human Clones and the Law.* New York: Cambridge University Press, 2005.

Barbara MacKinnon, ed.   *Human Cloning: Science, Ethics, and Public Policy.* Urbana: University of Illinois Press, 2000.

Jane Maienschein   *Whose View of Life? Embryos, Cloning, and Stem Cells.* Cambridge, MA: Harvard University Press, 2003.

Glenn McGee   *The Perfect Baby: Parenthood in the New World of Cloning and Genetics.* Lanham, MD: Rowman & Littlefield, 2000.

Glenn McGee and Arthur Caplan, eds.   *The Human Cloning Debate.* Berkeley, CA: Berkeley Hills Books, 2004.

Ann B. Parson	*The Proteus Effect: Stem Cells and Their Promise for Medicine.* Washington, DC: Joseph Henry Press, 2004.
Gregory E. Pence	*Cloning After Dolly: Who's Still Afraid?* Lanham, MD: Rowman & Littlefield, 2002.
President's Council on Bioethics	*Human Cloning and Human Dignity.* New York: Public Affairs, 2002. (Also available online at www.bioethics.gov/reports/ cloningreport.)
Michael Ruse and Aryne Sheppard, eds.	*Cloning: Responsible Science or Technomadness?* Amherst, NY: Prometheus Books, 2001.
Scientific American	*Understanding Cloning.* New York: Warner Books, 2002.
Stanley Shostak	*Becoming Immortal: Combining Cloning and Stem-Cell Therapy.* Albany: State University of New York Press, 2002.
Wesley J. Smith	*Consumer's Guide to a Brave New World.* San Francisco: Encounter Books, 2004.
United States House of Representatives Committee on Energy and Commerce	*Issues Raised by Human Cloning Research.* Honolulu, HI: University Press of the Pacific, 2005.
United States Senate Committee on the Judiciary	*Human Cloning: Must We Sacrifice Medical Research in the Name of a Total Ban.* Honolulu, HI: University Press of the Pacific, 2005.

Brent Waters and Ronald Cole Turner, eds.	*God and the Embryo: Religious Voices on Stem Cells and Cloning.* Washington, DC: Georgetown University Press, 2003.
Michael D. West	*The Immortal Cell.* New York: Doubleday, 2003.
Ian Wilmut	*The Second Creation: Dolly and the Age of Biological Control.* New York: Farrar, Straus & Giroux, 2000.

Periodicals

Douglas Allchin	"Genes 'R' Us," *American Biology Teacher*, April 2005.
Peter Berkowitz	"The Pathos of the Kass Report," *Policy Review*, October 2002.
Nell Boyce	"Is a Baby Clone on Board?" *U.S. News & World Report*, December 30, 2002.
Nell Boyce and James N. Pethokoukis	"Clowns or Cloners?" *U.S. News & World Report*, January 13, 2003.
Nell Boyce and Katherine Hobson	"Pets of the Future," *U.S. News & World Report*, March 11, 2002.
Linda Bren	"Cloning: Revolution or Evolution in Animal Production?" *FDA Consumer*, May 2003.
Alec Cawley	"Betting on Clone," *New Scientist*, October 30, 2004.
Kyla Dunn	"Cloning Trevor," *Atlantic Monthly*, June 2002.

Michael B. Farrell	"Cloning Kitty," *Christian Science Monitor*, November 24, 2004.
Thoman Fields-Meyer and Debbie Seaman	"Send in the Clones," *People*, September 8, 2003.
Tim Friend	"The Real Face of Cloning," *USA Today*, January 17, 2003.
Robert P. George and Patrick Lee	"Acorns and Embryos," *New Atlantis*, Fall 2004.
Nancy Gibbs et al.	"Abducting the Cloning Debate," *Time*, January 13, 2003.
Nancy Gibbs et al.	"Baby, It's You! And You, And You," *Time*, February 19, 2001.
Jerome Groopman	"Holding Cell," *New Republic*, August 5, 2002.
Lawrence M. Hinman	"The Ethics of Cloning Pets," *Los Angeles Times*, August 28, 2004.
Erik Jonietz	"Cloning, Stem Cells, and Medicine's Future," *Technology Review*, June 2003.
Daniel J. Kevles	"Cloning Can't Be Stopped," *Technology Review*, June 2002.
Arlene Judith Klotzko	"There'll Never Be Another You," *Guardian*, January 22, 2004.
Charles Krauthammer	"Crossing Lines," *New Republic*, April 29, 2002.
Brian Lavendel	"Jurassic Ark," *Animals*, Summer 2001.

Michael D. Lemonick et al.	"The Rise and Fall of the Cloning King," *Time*, January 9, 2006.
David Longtin and Duane C. Kraemer	"Cloning Red Herrings," *Policy Review*, February 2002.
James McManus	"Please Stand By While the Age of Miracles Is Briefly Suspended," *Esquire*, August 2004.
James Meek	"Tears of a Clone," *Guardian*, April 19, 2002.
Gregory Mone	"Invasion of the Clones," *Popular Science*, January 2005.
Ramesh Ponnuru	"Lapse of Reason," *National Review*, February 11, 2002.
David Quammen	"Clone Your Troubles Away: Dreaming at the Frontiers of Animal Husbandry," *Harper's*, February 2005.
Alan Richman	"Cloning Elvis," *Gentlemen's Quarterly*, May 2002.
Wade Roush	"Genetic Savings and Clone: No Pet Project," *Technology Review*, March 2005.
Michael J. Sandel	"The Case Against Perfection," *Atlantic Monthly*, April 2004.
Michael Shermer	"Wake Up, Cloning's Day Has Come," *Los Angeles Times*, January 2, 2003.
Wesley J. Smith	"It Didn't Start with Dolly," *Weekly Standard*, May 2, 2005.

Lisa Stein	"Cloned Food," *U.S. News & World Report*, November 10, 2003.
Gregory Stock and Francis Fukuyama	"The Clone Wars," *Reason*, June 2002.
Dawn Stover	"What You're Not Being Told About Cloning," *Popular Science*, December 2003.
Shannon A. Thomas	"Human Cloning," *America*, February 18, 2002.
Josh Ulick	"How to Make a Stem Cell," *Newsweek*, October 25, 2004.
Luba Vangelova	"True or False? Extinction Is Forever," *Smithsonian*, June 2003
Nicholas Wade and Choe Sang-Hun	"Human Cloning Was All Faked, Koreans Report," *New York Times*, January 10, 2006.
Linton Weeks	"Purr. Whirr," *Washington Post*, April 24, 2005.
Saul Weidensaul	"Raising the Dead," *Audubon*, May 2002.
Robert A. Weinberg	"Of Clones and Clowns," *Atlantic Monthly*, June 2002.
Ian Wilmut	"The Moral Imperative for Human Cloning," *New Scientist*, February 21, 2004.
Alan Zarembo	"$50,000 Cloned Kitten Truly Isn't One of a Kind," *Los Angeles Times*, December 23, 2004.

Index